# MOVING FORWARD FROM BEREAVEMENT

## OVERCOMING GRIEF AFTER THE LOSS OF A SPOUSE

### SANDRA CAMPONOGARA

# CONTENTS

*I dedicate this book to Marcelo. I know your soul is out there giving this book your Mona Lisa smile. Te amo. I wish you happiness in your next life.*

*Also, to everyone else who has grieved so deeply they felt they would never recover—this book is for you as well. I hope my story convinces you that you will learn to live again.*

# ACKNOWLEDGMENTS

To Marcelo, my high school sweetheart, thank you for a love story that will always live on.

To Jorge Fajardo and my amazing children, Ivan and Sabina, your steadfast support means the world to me. Thank you for your encouragement.

To Nadine Wills, my heartfelt thank you for helping me bring this project to life.

To Senator Bill Eigel, I am eternally grateful to you for donating bone marrow to Marcelo. You made it possible for our family to share eight more meaningful years together.

To Airam da Silva, President of the Icla da Silva Foundation, thank you for guiding us through the most challenging time in our lives and for your emotional support to our family. I am humbled by your tireless efforts to recruit bone marrow donors for life-saving transplants.

To Marcelo's excellent medical team at Hackensack University Medical Hospital, thank you for providing outstanding and compassionate care.

To all my wonderful friends, I owe my resilience to your support and encouragement. I thank you for lifting me up and always being in arm's reach when I need you. My children and I are blessed to have you in our lives.

**My gift**
*To You!*

# THE HEALING JOURNAL
## 6 POWERFUL STRATEGIES TO HELP YOU COPE WITH GRIEF

>> Scan the QR to Download your free Healing Journal <<

# PROLOGUE

L osing a spouse is a difficult challenge that can take years to recover from. Some people never do. There is the stereotype of the widow who never stops wearing black and the widower who dies not long after his wife for no discernable reason, because it is easy to get stuck in loss and longing. I want to tell a different story. Of how I grieved for my husband for many years, and certainly still haven't let my love for him go, but didn't get stuck there even though there were definitely times I worried I might.

This book will tell you how I worked through the grief of losing my husband of thirty years; going from the unrelenting pain of my loss to a stronger self, living a fulfilling life. My intention in writing this is to create something that can accompany those who have lost a spouse. Grief is a complex process, and if you are reading this because you are grieving, I want to give you hope that things will get better and maybe even offer some tools as well, to help you on your journey.

## THE ONE I LOVED

My name is Sandra, and I met Marcelo when I was only fourteen. Just imagine what the two of us must have looked like! We lived in Argentina and met in the summer of 1977 at a Swim Club. I probably had feathered hair like Farrah Fawcett and wore too much lip gloss at the time. But who would have known, anyway, because my hair was always wet and plastered to my head that summer. I ignored him at first because he kept bossing me around and splashing me when I wouldn't talk to him.

If it had been any other country, I probably would have spent hours talking on the phone about him to my friends. Complaining about how annoying he was. But I couldn't. In Argentina, in the 1970s, no one had telephones yet. Can you believe it? It seems impossible in retrospect. It was such a different world that we grew up in.

My mother didn't even want Marcelo and me to go out at all. She thought I was too young. In some ways, we were. We dated for a couple of years but, initially, he often was more interested in playing soccer. We would often argue about silly things. I would get mad and punish him in all sorts of ways, mostly because he would spend more time playing soccer than hanging out with me.

After two years of dating, we broke up amicably just before I began college. I didn't see Marcelo for eight months after that. There was so much going on in my life, starting college and making so many new friends, that I didn't really miss him all that much at first, to be honest. But when we saw each other again later that year, we both knew we were supposed to be together. It was different the second time.

It hadn't been serious before, but when we reunited, it was. We had never considered saying "I love you" before, but then suddenly there was no question we did. We knew we were going to get married. We knew we were going to spend our lives together. At least that's what we thought, as optimistic eighteen- and nineteen-year-olds. My mother still wasn't sure.

She was probably right to worry. But after that initial time apart, we stayed together, got married, moved to the US, and had two children. Marcelo became an engineer and I, after working in the tourism industry and raising our children, opened a travel business.

Our life was good and we had a loving relationship. It wasn't perfect, of course, but we complemented each other. We were happy with our life together in New Jersey. Even towards the end, in those final years when he was dying.

## BEFORE WE KNEW HE WAS GOING TO DIE

It feels strange to write that title, "Before we knew he was going to die." But there was a time when I was certain that I was going to be the first of us to go. I never thought about it very seriously though. Death had never touched us, or even our close family, until Marcelo got ill.

I don't think most people realize that they—or their loved ones—are actually going to pass away... until they do. Especially not someone like Marcelo. He was always so strong and athletic. Someone who seemed so healthy. Someone who would love me forever. Never leave me. Never die.

However, almost exactly thirty years after we first got together, we realized that something was wrong. In 2007, athletic, healthy, strong Marcelo finally admitted that he wasn't feeling well. I know some people joke about "man-flu" but Marcelo had never been like that. He was never one to complain about his health. Even when he did get hurt or had something wrong, he would usually figure out a way to patch himself up, and just get on with things. I think it was the engineer in him.

"Sandra, I've booked an appointment to see a doctor," he told me one day in 2007. I had been bugging him for months to do it, but never thought he would.

"Is this a joke? Are you sure it's not something you can fix yourself?" I laughed when he first told me, not really thinking about how serious or worried he must be if he was finally going to see someone. In all our time together, I can only remember him having gone to a doctor twice before.

When he said he was going to get some tests, I decided to go with him. I quickly understood that he wouldn't be going unless he thought he needed some further information he couldn't get himself, or wanted verification of something he thought he already knew. That's just the way he was. He must have figured it out, understood it was likely serious, and wanted evidence so they could find the best way to treat it.

He had been making some comments about being tired and having recurring and unusual aches and pains for some time, which is why I had started suggesting he go see a doctor. Honestly though, I had just assumed it was stress. Obviously, you know since you're reading this book that it wasn't. He had cancer.

I know he's not the only one to get that diagnosis or die from it. Many people experience the same shocking diagnosis and then the devastating ups and downs, struggle, and final, eventual death. Because die, he did. I suppose I started grieving while he was ill, but he was still there, so the grief didn't start seriously until he was gone. Then my journey with grief truly began.

I didn't feel as if I had just lost a spouse, though. I really felt as if I had lost part of myself. I lost our relationship. I lost my life. And I would never get any of those things back. I had to grieve and let go of all those things. Not just Marcelo. Marcelo first, of course. But slowly, I began to realize that I had lost all those other things as well. I had to honor and grieve those other losses as well and could not truly rebuild until I recognized that.

## TWO HALVES

We met young and then grew up together. You could say, in some ways, that we really became two halves of a whole. I knew that I could rely on him to take care of all the things he excelled in. Which meant I often never developed those parts of myself because he did that for us. And vice versa.

I always remember, for example, how organized Marcelo was. I am a reasonably neat person, but he was always more tidy. He was also the type of person who kept a file on everything. He never threw boxes or receipts away. Not even for something as small as our electric can opener from the 90s.

Instead, he spent hours storing everything away in our carefully organized attic with boxes lined up in sections that corresponded to the room we used them in. I see now that he was trying as hard as he could to make sure everything in our house worked and was safe. Because those two things were important to him.

Every gadget or electrical device we got was carefully unpacked. He would not only save its box, but every piece of packaging as well. He would then read through the instructions and ensure the warranty had been activated. Next, he always set up a folder for it, typing out its label like a very efficient secretary, and then filed its receipt first. I mean, who does that?

I used to complain that he was wasting the precious hours of our weekend together. Which seems silly now, in retrospect. I didn't see how much of a labor of love it was, how every single moment he spent doing that was, in his engineering mindset, a way of loving us. I wish I still had him here "wasting" his hours, creating those files.

And, because Marcelo loved to take care of everything related to instructions and electronics, I had nothing to do with things like that. Although I was involved in things that I saw as important, such as our finances, I never asked questions and trusted him completely when it came to putting our gadgets together and keeping their information stored.

Even more than figuring out how things worked, Marcelo liked making sure they were safe and would continue to work. Some people are natural mechanics. Marcelo was more of a natural quality assurance kind of guy. Which made him a great husband, actually. I knew I was safe with him. That he would do everything he could to ensure we all were safe. Unfortunately, he just forgot to do the same for himself…..

It was easy to let him do all the "safety" jobs when he was alive because he also enjoyed doing them. It did make some areas of my life more difficult afterwards, though. There were certain things I had never done because they were things Marcelo loved to do.

I know many couples are like this. If one person excels at something, then they take ownership of that in the relationship. It becomes "theirs." That's why if the couple gets divorced, or one dies, it can be such a shock. It's not just dealing with grief that can be diffi-cult, but learning to become whole again (or even for the first time, as with me) that can be an even greater task.

It seems like such a tiny thing, but in my experience, grieving and learning to live again are full of tiny moments that create many complex emotions. My intention in writing this book is to share my personal journey with death and grief, to explore all those hidden experiences I didn't find explained or shared elsewhere.

Like learning to be safe. After Marcelo died, I realized that I didn't have the built-in safety valve most adults do. I had to learn to be more careful since Marcelo wasn't playing that role for me in our lives anymore. It sounds like such a small thing, but it felt very large when I was grieving. I had to learn to take care of myself again.

I want to share these experiences, both large and small, to hopefully provide some of the information and inspiration I wish I had more of, when I was going through that process myself. I also want to help others to move forward (rather than using the term "move on") and consider how they can accomplish that in their own time and on their own terms.

It took Marcelo years to die from cancer. It was a long death, during which I often had to helplessly watch from his bedside as my partner struggled to keep every piece of his life till the end. It was devastating for both of us in many ways. There were good periods when he felt better, and we were able to live and love those years with each other, and as a family, as fully as possible.

These pages offer a safe space to feel the immensity of your (and my) grief and explore the potentialities hiding beyond pain. I respectfully offer ideas that have worked for me and others to alleviate the pain of bereaved hearts. Possibility awaits, and we can emerge on the other side of loss a stronger, wiser, more compassionate person. This book honors pain but also celebrates the wisdom and new types of happiness you can develop, even if grief strips your life of all the joy and things you loved before.

1

---

# THE FLOOD: WHAT GRIEF
# LOOKS LIKE

No one really understands grief until they feel it.
Many of us have watched others grieve. That
doesn't help you understand how it feels, though. Not
really. We know what grief *looks* like because there are
all sorts of stereotypes and rituals around death.

I thought I understood grief before it happened to me
because I had watched people I knew cry in public and
fall apart at strange times in those first couple of
months after they lost someone. Then, slowly, I saw
them swallow it until they somehow stopped grieving
so obviously.

Maybe that is part of the mourning process. Or, maybe
they just didn't feel comfortable sharing their ongoing

feelings anymore and learned to hide them. When it happened to me, that's what I learned to do after a time.

*Grief* is the initial reaction to loss (be it physical, emotional, mental, or social). *Mourning* is more about what you do in order to adapt to loss: it can be a personal response but often also encompasses cultural practices and rituals.

In contrast, *bereavement* is about time: the period of loss that includes both the grief and mourning processes. Mostly, in the beginning of this book, I talk about grief. Towards the end, I will start talking more about mourning.

In my experience, grief comes in waves and lasts for years. I didn't realize that before Marcelo died. I thought that someone died, you got sad and cried a lot and then eventually, maybe slowly, got better and moved on.

I also didn't understand that maybe you never let them go. At least not completely. That maybe their presence in your life, and then their death, changes you so much that tears are not enough to wash them out of your life.

For many people who lose a spouse, bereavement is a deep process that turns you inside out and takes years. That's something that no one ever seems to warn you about. Or at least, no one told me. No one told me that recovering yourself and your life after your spouse dies is not just about being sad and then not being sad. It's so much more horrible, and beautiful at the same time.

Because with deep grief comes a sort of dark wisdom I never thought I'd have. I still wish I hadn't gone through it, but since I did, I can now accept my dark wisdom as a gift for what I went through.

## GRIEVING TEETH

My body often took over my grieving in ways I never could have predicted. When I first learned that Marcelo had cancer, and was likely going to die, I found I couldn't breathe. I couldn't get any air at all and the doctors briefly had to turn all their attention to me in order to help me while I was processing the seriousness of the situation.

Similar things happened to my body when I was grieving. When it wasn't tears, my body would start to hurt. I had a series of strange temporary illnesses that initially terrified and tortured me until I learned that they were clearly psychosomatic. My body found ways to grieve if I wouldn't let it cry.

For example, after Marcelo's Celebration of Life service, I decided to drive down to Florida with my children and Marcelo's mother, who was staying with me. It was a two-day drive, which I had done before because I loved being down there. As I was driving, less than a week after his passing, I suddenly got a splitting headache.

I had never felt anything similar before. It felt as if half of my head was about to explode. I couldn't tolerate light anymore either.

It got so bad that I called my doctor back in New Jersey and said, "Look, we're driving through this town now, so could you please send something to the pharmacy here. I cannot stand it anymore. I'll pick it up here. But you need to send me the strongest medicine that you have because this is such a strong headache that it reaches down to my throat and frankly I cannot bear it."

My children had to take over the driving because the headache didn't go away, not on that trip or in the weeks after. It stayed for the next month, over Christmas, moving between my throat and my head until it eventually turned into a toothache that got so bad that on December 31st I found myself desperately searching for dentists who might be open.

I remember searching the web for someone who would be willing to see me on New Year's Eve and help me with my pain. It seemed a coincidence at the time, but it was the first New Year's Eve I was going to spend without Marcelo. It was a holiday we had always loved celebrating together. In fact, it was our favorite time of the year. Perhaps, there was also something in me that refused to let me be alone and in pain. Maybe that was part of it.

All I knew was that I couldn't bear the pain and I needed help. I found a dentist who was open and told him, "I have so much pain on this side of my face that I need you to take out my teeth or something. I don't know what it is but I need you to take my pain away."

The dentist took some X-rays, examined them, came back and told me, "You have nothing wrong with your teeth. Everything seems to be okay. I can't find anything. I don't think there is a problem."

"I don't care," I said. "I want you to do something. Do a root canal or take it out or do something with me. I want you to fix it. I need you to take my pain away."

So they did. They did a root canal that I technically didn't need. I look back on that now and can see that going to the dentist was maybe partially me seeking someone to play a role similar to the one Marcelo had always played in my life. He fixed everything. More importantly, when he was alive he was always watching over me, trying to ensure I was safe.

It was strange that he wasn't around telling me to be careful or warning me about something or giving me things to help take care of me. And now that I was in pain, and needed his care more than I ever had, I felt his absence more than ever.

He had always found ways to keep me safe and was always watching over me to make sure I wasn't hurt or in pain. Maybe that's why, as soon as I lost him, my body started protesting as a way to try to summon him back. It knew that he would be so upset that I was hurt that if anything would bring him back, that would. But it didn't.

So what I did in response is that I went from dentist to dentist, trying to find him by asking them to fix my phantom pain. And none of them could. None of them were him. None of them knew that what I really wanted them to do was bring Marcelo back. Or for them to hold my face lovingly the way he used to and gaze into my eyes, which used to give me such a feeling of safety and being cherished.

I didn't know at the time that's what I really wanted, either. That is what I now think my body was trying to tell me, though. I misunderstood and instead desperately tried to dig the pain out with root canal after root canal. I ended up having five root canals in total. All completely unnecessary. Or maybe they were necessary. Maybe it was a horribly necessary way I needed to mourn my lost love. With laughing gas.

For people who have never been through deep, traumatic grief, it would be very easy to judge this as a bit crazy. But, I am certain that anyone who has known this type of pain understands the downward spiral and dark places that deep grief leads you towards. The inexplicable places that are so easy to label as problematic from the outside, but in some ways, when my mind and heart weren't able to heal themselves yet, my body was trying to take over. It was shouting at me that I needed to get this out of me somehow. That I needed to keep digging and poking at it and getting help until something worked.

What I needed was to grieve. Books and movies portray grief in such stereotyped and tame ways. A couple of tears. A month or two. But it's not like that. Not in my experience or that of the people I've known who have told me about theirs. It splits you open until you think you are never going to be able to put yourself or your life back together again. Until you don't even recognize yourself anymore and you are crawling desperately and wailing on the floor in defeat and fear and suffering.

My emotional pain felt overwhelmingly immense and the physical pain I felt echoed that as well, so I needed a solution that was just as powerful. Eventually, the incredible intensity of that initial pain subsided and that's when I stopped needing to get root canals.

Initially, I think I had all those root canals because I wanted Marcelo back. During that period, I was in almost constant pain; it would migrate between my head, teeth and throat and it lasted about a year. Looking back, I suppose in some ways, that pain was about me not being able to fully express my grief and wanting Marcelo to care for me during my bereavement.

That experience was so painful that I was willing to pay people to try to pry it out of me instead. Perhaps, not coincidentally, that pain lasted almost exactly a year following Marcelo's death.

## WEARING MARCELO'S BODY

It's perhaps then not surprising that the holiday season following my root canals, I found myself having ailments that Marcelo had always had. It was as if my body was also trying to bring him back again by remembering the tiny pains he sometimes had. The acid reflux. His sore knee. I had started going to yoga and told my teacher. She suggested that maybe I should try to heal it or do whatever I would have told Marcelo to do.

I can still remember rummaging through our medicine cabinet after going home from yoga, crying again, collecting up the last bits of his medication. Not his cancer pills, as I threw all those out immediately after he died, but the things he kept to heal himself. The Pepto Bismol I would scold him for drinking too much of. The bandage he used to wrap his knee with.

It was a miserable winter Saturday, not long before the second Christmas after his death. I spent the afternoon drinking tiny sips from his old, crusty Pepto Bismol bottle with his tension bandage wrapped around my knee, crying, and saying goodbye to him, yet another time.

There were many times like that. So many times when I thought he was gone from my life, but then my body would remind me that I loved him and missed him and that I still had grief I had to pay attention to. It was frustrating, but my body wouldn't let me ignore it.

I think it was after my Pepto Bismol session that I realized that I probably needed to find others. People who understood that grieving often lasts beyond a couple of months. After about six months, most people in my life seemed to assume I would be fine. Or, at least, they didn't seem to want to see me grieving anymore.

That's when I started becoming ashamed of my grief. Of my tears. Of my body exploding with sadness. Eventually, I found my way to books and online communities where other people shared their stories about how long their grief lasted and how it appeared in their bodies and lives.

What a relief it was to connect with them and read their stories. I began to understand that bereavement is different for everyone but also often goes in cycles. That our minds, emotions and bodies will have an immediate reaction and then a series of reactions over time as we heal.

## LETTING GO OF MY "HOME"

I realized grief is a much deeper and longer journey than I had ever imagined when I sold our home four years after Marcelo died. I wasn't even living there anymore, having already moved to Florida, but I still needed to say goodbye to my life there when I finally sold the house.

Although I had mourned him fully in many ways, had gone through all the stages and was living life again to some extent, I still saw him as my home and the place and person who kept my heart. Marcelo was very connected to our house in my memories, which is why, when I sold it, I needed to grieve again.

I didn't realize that I still had to "move out" and let go of him being where I lived, so to speak. It was only when I actually began the process of selling the home where we had lived that a whole deeper level of grief hit me and I had to go through grieving him all over again, in a way.

At each "first" that I lived through without him, I would start hoping, "Is this the end? Am I going to wake up tomorrow and be the old Sandra again? Will I get my life back soon?" But I never did. Part of me selling our home was accepting I never would.

So, when I finally decided to sell our home in New Jersey, I had to grieve for him all over again because Marcelo was so connected to that house in my mind. It was the house we had raised our children in. But when I saw the house, I saw him. It just was *his* house in a way, and I felt that it held a part of him. I suppose I was also grieving the life I was leaving behind in it, as well.

Marcelo had always been interested in alternative energy sources and so put solar panels onto our house much earlier than most people. His engineering background made it a point of pride for him to ensure they worked well and efficiently, which ended up being a very attractive selling point when I finally wanted to sell it.

However, like I mentioned before, that was his thing and something I had never paid attention to. I don't know anything about solar panels. Not about how they work or exactly how efficient they were or how they work on cloudy days.

Of course, the prospective buyers were asking questions and needed the specific information and facts about them before the closing. I had not participated in the solar panel project because that was Marcelo's baby.

In short, I had nothing on the solar panels to give to the buyers. But I knew he was very organized so for the first time since he died, I opened his computer and found his 'solar panel folder' with all the information I needed. Although I felt like a hacker, breaking into his most personal things, I knew he would have a folder like that. He did. Of course he did.

Oh, Marcelo and his folders! I remember how it used to annoy me that he spent so much time on his folders. I felt a tear begin to slowly drip down my cheek.

"Don't start," I muttered to myself. "If you start, you'll sit here crying all day." And with that, I started wailing. I cried. And cried some more because I missed him making all those folders.

I looked at his folders and realized that I wasn't only sad, though. At that moment, I was sad and proud. I missed that part of "me" which was our perfectly balanced relationship. The part I felt at home in. The part of me I knew so well and had trusted, and then had lost and couldn't seem to find again.

Marcelo used to have such a big capacity to handle both big and small projects with ease. I loved that about him. It made me feel safe whenever I felt overwhelmed, and I felt overwhelmed now. If he was here, finding information on solar panels wouldn't have fazed him at all. He certainly wouldn't be sitting in front of a computer crying at folders.

I realized that seeing his folders was like seeing him again, in a way. It put me right back into grieving. I needed to stop everything and cry and let all those emotions come up and recognize how sad I was that he was not here with me anymore. I sat there crying for a long time, stroking the screen. Perhaps, that was my way of saying goodbye to the part of him that still resided in that house.

Eventually, the tears stopped. As opposed to some of the other times I'd been overwhelmed with grief, what I could feel as well was that I was grateful for our lives together and for the amazing children we raised together. I got up and walked around the home we had shared together. I remembered all the photos of us that had hung on those walls, documenting our life together, and the bookshelves we used to have stuffed with souvenirs from vacations. I realized that when I went back to Florida, he would not be moving there with me after all. Part of him was staying here.

I was finally leaving home, in a way. Because we had gotten together so young, and he was older than me and so very competent, I had never had to take my own first wobbly steps alone in the world without him. That's part of why I had to go through another stage of grief at my computer.

His folders had always been so symbolic of the care he put into our lives together and into our family. After I left New Jersey, he would still be in my heart, but he would no longer be my home in the same way. No longer someone who had built solar panels and papered almost every inch of the space we shared. Selling our house made it obvious that, in the future, he would no longer be my home, but only someone I visited in my memory.

Everyone expresses grief in their own time, and in often unexpected ways through their bodies, and it often goes on for much longer than you or others expect it should.

# 2

# THE GOODBYE: WAS IT A GOOD DEATH?

Aside from the cause of death, the atmosphere within which someone dies, where they die and whether their loved ones are able to be with them, can all affect whether or not someone has what they, or their loved ones, feel is a good death.

The circumstances of the death also have an effect on the bereavement of those they leave behind. If it is death after a long illness, like it was with Marcelo, that changes the grief process significantly. Perhaps ironically, though, when he finally died, it felt sudden for us. He caught pneumonia and died unexpectedly. He had been relatively well, going through a stable period.

We were confident, at that point, that we could expect him to survive for significantly longer. And then, suddenly he caught pneumonia and had to be admitted into hospital and never left. Instead of getting better as we kept expecting him to, he just died. It may seem silly to others that his death caught us by surprise, but it did.

People who die young or by suicide are mourned differently than others because their deaths are usually a surprise as well. Generally, the circumstances and environment surrounding a death can greatly affect how it is grieved. Many people know this from personal experience because of the pandemic.

During COVID, many people had loved ones die without a chance to say goodbye in person or being able to give them any proper farewell rituals. Similarly, this often happens during wars and natural disasters.

I lost my mother at the beginning of the pandemic. She was ill at home but isolated from all extended family. That meant we could not have a funeral for her, which we all experienced as deeply painful and which added another layer to our grief and suffering after her death.

In each of those situations, death is treated differently, and so expectations of what a good death is changes depending upon each circumstance as well.

DEATH ROW

Sometimes we have to help our loved ones process their mortality, upcoming death and its mysteries so that they can feel free, finally, to let go. The moment we found out about Marcelo's cancer actually foreshadowed how both Marcelo and I would continue to deal with his cancer and death going forward.

Marcelo was very matter-of-fact about the whole experience, often almost to the point of being emotionless, wanting to focus on details and numbers instead as a way of getting through it. I, on the other hand, often got easily overwhelmed by grief, and my emotions often migrated into my body and became psychosomatic pain. So, it was natural that I began acting out psychosomatically some of the grief that Marcelo felt.

It was July 1, 2008 when Marcelo was supposed to get the results from some blood tests. He had been feeling pain for a long time without any obvious explanation. We knew there was something wrong, but still didn't expect the news we got. At least I didn't. Looking back now, I suppose Marcelo's reaction could be explained by the fact that he did. I went with him to his appointment but when we arrived, we noticed that there were three other doctors in the room waiting for us.

They were all sitting behind desks, staring at us with serious looks on their faces. They weren't chatting with each other. They weren't looking at their notes impatiently. They weren't doing anything. Not moving. They didn't smile or get up to shake our hands or even say "hello" as they usually would at the beginning of an appointment. It wasn't a good start.

Marcelo leaned over to me and whispered into my ear, "I feel like I'm on death row."

I grabbed his hand and tried to cheer him up a little bit by saying, "You don't know for sure that it is going to be bad news. Sometimes doctors need other specialists in the room to consult or to explain the results. Just remember, you don't know for sure. Let's just wait and see."

I bit my lip though, and noticed that my breath started to speed up. We sat down beside each other in tandem at exactly the same time. After so many years together, we often did things in harmony like that.

Without any further introduction or small talk, Dr. Goldberg gave us the results. "Well, we have studied your results and you have A-L-L. That is a type of cancer. It's leukemia actually. And it is serious. It's a very aggressive case."

Marcelo listened. He thought for a moment and then said he wanted to get a second opinion. I'll never forget Dr. Goldberg's response.

He looked Marcelo straight in the eye and said, "There is no time for another opinion."

## SYMBIOTIC LUNGS

Marcelo was focused and matter of fact about it. He wanted to know statistics and get as much information as he could. My breath got faster and faster. The room was getting hotter. My lungs felt as if they were getting smaller and it was all I could do to breathe. I couldn't listen anymore. I just had to focus on gasping in air.

Marcelo wanted to know what his options were, such as a bone marrow transplant if a donor became available, when he needed to start chemotherapy, and what other treatments would be needed.

As they continued to talk, I started hyperventilating. I tried to take deep breaths and eventually got up and walked over to the window to look out at the parking lot. Dr. Goldberg stopped giving facts to Marcelo at one point to make sure I was okay. Of course I wasn't. Marcelo had cancer and he was going to die. I couldn't breathe.

From that point, after Dr. Goldberg told us "There is no time for another opinion," our life changed forever. Everything would happen so fast, that by the July 4th weekend, Marcelo had already been admitted into hospital to begin his treatments.

How we both responded so very differently to that experience predicted how the next eight years would continue. In some ways, within the context of our relationship, I carried the burden of expressing both our emotions and grief about his diagnosis. While, in many other ways, Marcelo coped and dealt with all the details in order to ensure that we continued to function practically.

I think, looking back, that this meant that my body or my feelings sometimes expressed the grief he never explicitly did because it needed to try to focus on surviving instead. But, it also meant that even though I knew he was dying for eight years, some of my own grief was put on hold because I was ensuring that he had a "good death" with this sort of strange, unspoken symbiosis.

And, because in some ways he had often expressed his emotions through me and my body, I did that for him one last time while he was dying. That started most obviously at his doctor's appointment when he got his diagnosis. I think he was able to stay so calm because I was panicking for both of us, in a way.

I continued to emotionally caretake, and be his surrogate griever in many ways, while he focused on life over the next eight years so that he could still find ways to express the feelings he wouldn't have otherwise had the energy to experience.

I don't want to suggest that Marcelo couldn't express his emotions. He was very loving, expressive and charming. He certainly expressed his own emotions in his own ways as well, it's just that having grown up together and having been partnered for thirty years, this was one way we had learned to balance each other, and how I sometimes functioned in our relationship during crisis. So that is one way, although it wasn't obvious, I supported him—and I think many women do this for their husbands as a sort of invisible "work" to help them process things they otherwise wouldn't. This continued while he was dying as well.

I remember when we got back into the car after the appointment, Marcelo looked over at me. I thought he might start crying or say something sad but he didn't.

"I knew it. That *was* Death Row. The only time in my life I've ever had any real intuition and it had to be then."

We both sat and stared at all the cars moving back and forth around us and then started laughing and couldn't stop for a long time. Longer than the joke was funny, because we didn't know what else to do. Eventually we had to leave or risk getting a parking ticket.

## A GOOD DEATH?

Although the doctors initially thought that Marcelo possibly only had weeks or months to live when they gave him his diagnosis, in the end, he lived eight years. Some of those weeks and months were better than others. Sometimes he was almost independent and would feel almost normal for a time. But it never lasted long; he weakened and wasted away, and became increasingly dependent on his nurses and me towards the end.

I won't tell every detail of how Marcelo died, but I was proud of how he and we coped with the situation and his dying. So, in that way, we were able to remain united as a family unit. Towards the end, he moved into the hospital because of pneumonia, which was a real surprise to us all, as I mentioned before. We didn't think that was what would eventually get him.

He was there for forty days struggling to recover. We just kept thinking he would get better, including the doctors, but he never did. I spent every one of those days with him and I'm glad I did, because even up until a couple of days before he passed, we didn't realize how serious it had gotten.

Through all of Marcelo's struggling and surviving and dying, I was there with him every step of the way. I'm proud of how I cared for and accompanied him. When he was scared, when he needed help, and then in his last hours when I could almost see his soul give up and something change, as if it had decided to leave his body.

I don't know what other people mean by a "good death." Maybe they mean that it is painless. Marcelo didn't get that. He experienced pain and struggle during the years of his battle against cancer, but I still think he had a good death. Even though we had expected him to have more life than he did.

If you have watched someone who has been dying for a long time, you notice that they go through stages of letting go of life. They slowly disengage in various ways, physically, mentally, emotionally, bit by bit, until they are ready to let go altogether. Marcelo went through this process in a very condensed way in the last day or so of his life.

He became so still in those last days that he rarely moved or talked much anymore. Even when I held his hand and stroked his hair, he barely moved anymore. He often couldn't even open his eyes to look at me anymore or squeeze my hand back in response.

However, while heavily sedated he moved his mouth very slightly into—what I called—a Mona Lisa smile on two occasions. Very few other people would have noticed but we, and I in particular, had spent so many hours staring at his face over the years and during those last days that we saw. We knew when it was more than a twitch. We knew when he was communicating something.

So, even when heavily sedated, he somehow understood when his mother was finally able to come from Argentina, and walked into the room. She was so happy to understand that, even in those last moments, he was able to communicate his love for her. The other was when his favorite song would start to play. Still, aside from those slight indications he was still alive somewhere in there, it was obvious that he was slipping away and no longer responded or was connected to us or the world as much anymore.

Even that ever-so-slight movement cost him great effort to leave wherever his soul had begun to fly away towards. Because that is what I believe was happening. His soul was leaving his body and beginning to see the beauty of another place and existence. I think he was sad to leave us, but that he was beginning to understand how beautiful the place he was going to was, while he waited to return to Earth. I think it's always more painful for the people who remain behind.

But he had a strong attachment to us and so his soul didn't want to leave even though it was going somewhere beautiful. I think he held on longer than he needed to. Just to stay with us longer. And I think it caused him pain, actually. That longing to be with us as long as possible.

Because he loved us so much he was willing to undergo a little bit of extra pain just to remain with us longer. Is that a good death or a bad death? I'm not sure exactly. But I'm so happy we were able to all be together in the way we were. We did the best we could under the circumstances and maybe that's all you can do in the end.

When exactly he died was hard to tell, because I didn't hear him breathe his last breath or sense his soul leaving or anything obvious like that. I think it was more as if his soul was slowly detaching from his body over that last day or so. However, after he was taken off the ventilator, his body died quickly. Suddenly, he stopped breathing. He was gone. After so many years of fighting to be with us, Marcelo was dead.

I think that because we ended up having so much more time than Dr. Goldberg had said to expect, we had stopped expecting him to die at any moment. We knew he was dying, but still were shocked that he died suddenly because he had been doing so well. It might sound strange to outsiders who knew he was terminally ill, but to us, he had been "healthy."

Still, we as a family had time to adjust to the fact he was going to leave us at some point and were able to say "I love you" and "goodbye" when we knew that it might be the last time we saw each other. Even if we were only leaving each other for a couple of hours. We just knew we had less time with him than we had realized previous to his diagnosis.

And, we were able to be there with him by his bedside in his last days. We were able to watch him slowly let go of fighting. Of life. Of us. Even of himself. It was heart-breaking, but that is death. And so, it was as good a death as death can be even if we didn't want him to leave us and didn't think it should have ever happened at all.

---

A good death may not be the calm, peaceful death we imagined and may turn out instead to be something very different, like channeling their pain or listening to them shout about how they aren't ready to die.

# 3

# THE TEST: BELIEFS ABOUT DEATH

I wish I had all the answers and knew without a shadow of a doubt what happens when we die. But I don't. For example, I can't say for certain what happened when Marcelo died, although I've already said I think his soul went to a better place while it waits to return to Earth. That's just me, over the years I've developed my own set of beliefs about death that include reincarnation.

## THE POINT OF DEATH

When we were waiting for Marcelo to die, I found out that doctors don't all agree on the exact moment of death, which surprises me. With Marcelo, it was obvious and very quick in terms of the physical moment he died. He had been distant and letting go in the days before but then he clearly "died."

That is not always true with everyone. For that reason, there are a number of different medical definitions. Some say it is when the heart stops beating. Others argue that no, that is too imprecise and that it is actually when the brain stops functioning. Even then there are arguments within arguments about different types of brain death and so on.

I expected the moment of death, at least medically, to be much more obvious. While most people in the medical community agree upon some general guidelines for declaring death, they also accept that these are imprecise. I thought that with all the machines they have in hospitals nowadays that they, at least, would be able to read and record death clearly. But it turns out they can't. Not always.

When someone is on a ventilator, like Marcelo was towards the end, and they shut that off, the body still continues on by itself for a while. It is only when the brain stops that the body slowly shuts down organ by organ. So, when do they actually die? Is it when every organ ceases or some time before that when the brain stops, because it is clear then they cannot survive and so are effectively dead for all intents and purposes?

I thought it would be much more precise. Doctors would usually declare it at the point when brain function stops I think, but it's not an exact science and is still debated. Beyond all the physical aspects, I'm not sure if any of that is what is really important, anyway. Because perhaps the body is just a shell. So, if the body is just a shell then when it stops, it is not the body that matters but the soul. The soul might not even leave the body at the same time that the body stops functioning but could stay around for a while. At least I think it might.

I think many people would agree that people are their "soul," at least as much or more so than their body. If that is true, then doctors have been measuring when the body dies but not when the "person" does. I don't know how you could measure a soul leaving the body. As far as I know, neither do science nor doctors yet either.

## LETTING GO

Looking back at those last eight years of his life, I wonder if Marcelo lived so much longer than he was supposed to because he needed more time to let go. Sometimes, I wonder if something happened in that last year that made him think, even subconsciously, that it was okay to finally leave.

He was someone who was so alive and loved so much and was so rooted here with us and to this Earth that maybe when he was called away, as I believe our souls are, it took him eight years to detach and respond to that summons. Maybe he had finally made all his good-byes or was convinced that we would be able to survive without him. I think that there were a number of things which he finally realized had happened in that last year which gave him peace.

For example, both our kids had finished college and my travel business had become more stable and successful. He was always worried that we wouldn't be able to take care of ourselves financially without him, I think, and really valued education, so once he was satisfied we were going to be okay, on some level he felt he could finally "leave."

I know his body died as I mentioned above, but I'm pretty certain his soul didn't leave immediately. He definitely "haunted" us for a while. Having learned and listened and read a lot about death in the past number of years, one of the things that has surprised me the most about it is how differently everyone interprets and understands the process of death.

In fact, it seems to me that everyone has slightly different beliefs about it. This seems true even when they are part of the same religion. Things like culture, country, personal experience and personality often influence beliefs about death.

For example, Marcelo and I grew up in the same area of Argentina, had very similar upbringings, fell in love and then shared our lives together from an early age. But we had very different understandings about death.

Although he knew he was going to die, Marcelo didn't care about a funeral and never wanted to talk about it much or organize anything in advance.

He said, "Sandra, I'm going to be dead. It's not up to me what you do. Just do something that you feel will help you and the kids after I'm gone. That's all I want. I don't even want a funeral. You know that Sandra. Baby, *cara*, if you do anything it should be for you. Do whatever you need to do as a family to remember me. Okay?"

I would never want people to have a funeral for me either, actually. I'm very much a "Celebration of Life" kind of woman. So, after he was gone, since he had given me his blessing to do whatever we wanted, and his mother and our kids agreed, we didn't have a funeral for him. We chose to give him a Celebration of Life because he had always been so lively. And he had fought death so hard.

We wanted our last memories we made with him to be about his life. We had him cremated and then took him up to a mountain where he had loved to hike. We had spent many hours there as a family, on weekends when the children were young. We spread his ashes and all shared our favorite memories about Marcelo. Things that we loved about him. Things we admired about him.

Sharing with each other why he had been such a beautiful friend, son, father and husband helped us let him die. We all talked about experiences with him we had never told anyone else before and that helped us know each other, and him, better. We bonded as a community of people who had loved and been part of Marcelo's life. It allowed us to start seeing how good he had been and how much good he had done in the world, and accept that it was maybe enough for now and that his "job" this time round was over.

So, he was right. The way we remembered him was more for us than him. It helped us give him a good death in a way we needed. Most people wouldn't think about it that way, because it wasn't important to Marcelo himself, but it was important to those who loved him. We needed to talk about him together one last time.

Marcelo could be logical and unemotional when he thought about his actual death. It's not that he wanted to die, not at all. He loved us and his life. But I don't think he really believed in anything after death and knew that we were the ones who would have to deal with him being gone.

Saying that would have killed his mother so he never said it too obviously, but that might have also been why he waited around here so long. He wanted to make sure he got in everything he needed to say and do, just in case. He wasn't sure he'd have another chance.

## SECOND CHANCES

I am pretty sure he will though. I believe that we come back to life throughout history. Many times. I think that it is pretty obvious that the body is a biological thing. It lives and dies and then that is it. And there is nothing further for the body per se.

However, I believe in an eternal soul. I think that we do come back to Earth to learn new things. We keep coming back to gather more experiences, to help improve ourselves and become better over time, aiming for perfection. This is something that we cannot achieve in one lifetime, which is why we need to keep coming back. I believe that.

Marcelo, as a person who has passed, is still a soul waiting somewhere "out there" for a new opportunity to return to Earth. However, I don't think he left immediately but that he stayed around us for a while.

Marcelo was the type of person you noticed. He had a big presence. He was hard to miss. He was tall and had a vibrant personality. He was friendly, had a lot of opinions and was always talking in a loud voice.

In our house, I always knew when he was at home because he made so much noise. I don't think Marcelo did anything quietly. We laughed about that fact many times, actually. I remember early on that we realized that he couldn't play the Tooth Fairy because he would wake the kids up. I remember giggling downstairs as I heard him trying to tiptoe into one of their rooms to slip money under their pillows, the first couple of times he insisted on trying.

It sounded like a herd of elephants crashing through a jungle. Every time he tipped a toe, it came crashing down thunderously. Stomping his way across their room, he tried to avoid toys strewn across the floor, like moving through an obstacle course in tap shoes. I started laughing so hard, I had to sit down on the kitchen floor, where I had been washing dishes, and just stare up at the ceiling shaking my head at him.

I never let him forget it and liked to tease him in front of people about it. Marcelo was good-natured and would laugh along. Loudly of course. So, when he died our house was suddenly much, much quieter.

Even though he had been in the hospital for over a month, it's as if his shadow had been keeping it warm and "noisy" somehow. And then, when he died, all his echoes just faded away. The difference from one day to the next felt incredibly stark.

Our home suddenly felt empty and silent when I returned. His ambient bangs and crashes and splutters and laughter had disappeared. I realized that he had provided a sort of background soundtrack for my life, and now that it had been turned off, everything felt wrong.

Until, at times, I would feel his presence again. Sometimes, I would be in a public place and think I heard his laugh or voice or his footsteps. It could have been someone else who sounded or moved like him. That probably was it occasionally, but sometimes, especially not long after he died, I had the feeling he was checking in on me.

It was immediately after he passed that I felt his presence the most. I'm not sure if it's because he hadn't fully left me yet or he was still making sure I would be okay and was coming back more often to see me. However, I would know he was there when I was alone, just the same way you would if your back was turned and someone you know well walked in the room without making a sound.

You're so tuned into some people that you can sense their energy. If they tiptoe up to you (and they're not Marcelo) and put their hands over your eyes and say, "Guess who?" if it's someone close, you often know. Maybe it's their smell or energy or a soul connection. I don't know. But it was that same knowing I used to have when he was alive and I knew he was near.

It never scared me to sense his presence back in the house after he had died. It felt comfortable and caring. He never stayed for long or spoke to me in any meaningful way. They were just brief visits. I could always guess the reason he was there as well. For example, he checked in a couple of times when I was in the kitchen cutting things with sharp knives.

Marcelo was always worried about me slipping and cutting myself with them. He was always very safety-oriented and I'm not. For that reason, when he saw me with a particular couple of knives when he was alive, he would often softly say, "If you worked in a factory, you would be walking around with three fingers on each hand."

He was trying to create some more awareness in me so that I would be more conscious about safety. After he died, the first couple of times I used those knives he used to warn me about, I could feel him there very strongly.

Even now, if I'm in the kitchen and forget what I'm doing and start handling a knife in an unsafe manner or burn a finger when I'm cooking, anything that potentially he would have tried to correct me about, I can almost hear him or feel him breathing on my neck. Now though, it's less of an actual presence and more of an apparition. A ghostly memory.

At first, it felt as if he was really there, but just invisible or around a corner. Now, when he appears, I'm not sure. It seems to me that sometimes it is still him but that he's definitely passed to another side so that he's far away, and there is some sort of curtain or distance between us. He's not as close as he once was, but I still feel his presence.

Because of those experiences though, I realize that he is still around. That his soul is still with me. At least sometimes. For now. Because of that, when I need to make a decision on little things that I previously would have consulted with him on, I still sometimes talk to him in my mind. I pretend that he's there with me.

I start off by asking myself, "If Marcelo was here, what would he do in this situation or advise me to do?"

I think it through, and as I imagine him thinking or doing and being in the situation, it's almost as if he appears alongside me. That's when I will turn to him.

I ask, "Should we do this or not? How are we going to go about this?"

That's what we would have done when he was alive. It was always easy that way between us. I always liked and valued the advice he gave me. So, from time to time, I even choose to go with the way that he would have chosen to handle a situation. That is one way that I keep his presence alive in my life and with me in my heart. Because I don't feel like I want to deny his presence and his wisdom in my life completely. And, that's one way that I sometimes choose to acknowledge him.

---

People have a range of beliefs about how we die and what happens to our souls after death, but I believe that the soul is eternal and we can sometimes feel the presence of those close to us who have passed.

# 4

# THE WREATH: REMEMBERING YOUR SPOUSE

I know that some people idolize their dead spouses in retrospect. After they're gone, it's easy to forget what they were like day-to-day, and all the times they were less than perfect. I never did that with Marcelo. Perhaps it was because we were lucky enough and happy enough. I know it is a rare gift that I didn't have to make up any fairy tales in order to get him to forgive me, or to forgive myself, once he was gone.

What I did struggle with, though, was trying to remember him. That sounds horrible! I know. I was with my husband for thirty years. How could I forget him? It doesn't even make sense to me. But it's true. Part of it was my mind trying to protect me I think, shutting down a part of my life that hurt to remember. Another was a pattern of mine. I've always been someone who's been more focused on the future than the past anyway. Marcelo used to joke that I would forget my name if it wasn't written on all my identification.

So, I had good reason to worry about forgetting him.. It was likely to happen because that's what I do: forget. I was terrified of beginning to lose the tiny details that made me love him. The things that no one else knew to remind me of because they were private moments and things we had only shared with each other.

Some things weren't even special, just those little things I didn't want to forget, like how he would never bother to sit down to put his pants on but would hop around trying to get both his legs into his pants at the same time. He would always almost fall over in the process. Every single time. Every single day. Of his life. What a silly, lovable man. My man. How could I forget that? But I already had begun in little bits and pieces.

Whenever I would smile at him hopping around trying to get his pants on, he would teasingly sing or whisper the line of a Spanish song to me in response. But I can no longer remember what it was. And no one else ever heard him do that so there is no one to help jog my memory. It's lost forever.

In our relationship, we were many things but in general, Marcelo was practical and organized and loud and I was nurturing and creative and forgetful. While sometimes being forgetful can be helpful in a long-term relationship, I didn't feel as if I could afford to be that way anymore. But I was already falling back into that pattern, which meant I was losing my Marcelo. How could I?

After his death, I wanted to do everything I could to keep him alive in my mind and heart and our family stories, so that neither me nor my children would forget him: his voice, the way he walked, his habits, the things he loved and hated, all the little things that can be so easy to forget if you don't share them. So, I tried to do everything I could. I wrote down little snippets on Post-it notes. I told my kids as many stories as I could. And now, I am writing this book.

Inevitably, you lose the one you love after they die. You can't keep them alive completely no matter how hard you try to hold on to their memory. You forget things and memories and keepsakes fade. I had to accept that this is part of the bereavement process.

Just as I watched Marcelo distance himself from us and let go of life, forgetting is part of the way I suppose my subconscious forced me to distance myself from him, and actually allows me to live life despite him being gone. I've learned that it doesn't mean I love him less, which was my initial fear; it just means that we're in different places now.

GHOST

When our children were small, the movie *Ghost* (Zucker, 1990) was popular. If I remember correctly, I think Marcelo and I even saw it on a date night. Amiably fighting each other for fistfuls of popcorn in the cinema, we watched as the Demi Moore character made pottery. Suddenly the ghost of her loving, dead husband appeared behind her.

"Oooooooooh," Marcelo leaned over and whispered in my ear.

"Shut up." I punched his arm. "He's being romantic. Try and learn something from him."

On-screen, the husband-ghost character played by Patrick Swayze hugged Demi Moore close as he tried to get her to feel his presence. He wanted her to remember his love and to not forget him. They made pottery to the tune of "Unchained Melody." It was beautiful. I wiped away a tear and hoped Marcelo hadn't noticed.

He had. Of course he had. I knew that Marcelo was looking at me and smiling in the dark. I felt his fingers on my cheek, wiping my tears away. He thought me crying at things like that was silly, but he knew I loved touching movies. That's why he chose that movie for me. That's why I was letting him get most of the popcorn as a thank-you.

Maybe Marcelo remembered us watching that film. Who knows? I'm not sure how many other people feel the presence of their dead spouse after they die. But Marcelo came back regularly for those first couple of years. We didn't make pottery together. Marcelo was never quite that romantic. Remember I said he was more of the quality assurance type of guy? Well, that's often how he showed his love for me. By appearing when he felt the need to warn me.

Not just when he worried about me though, but also on big occasions that related to our children. Times when we would have all been celebrating them together. I would often swear I felt him standing behind me clapping or smiling. Sending out loving energy to me and our family, wanting us to remember how much he loved us. Sort of like Patrick Swayze but with fewer muscles and more of an engineer's Health and Safety vibe.

CAGES

Something I noticed in the online forums, and with the widowed friends that I was beginning to develop, was that everyone reacted differently over time to losing their spouse and how they chose to remember them.

Those who had had a difficult relationship with the spouse who died often had more extreme reactions than others. For obvious reasons, they often either found a huge sense of relief (that they didn't want to express or admit to anyone) or guilt.

After sometimes years in toxic or abusive relationships, it was no wonder that many suddenly felt freed. However, this was not something that they were able to openly discuss with family and friends. They felt ashamed, and so often played at, and performed, a grief they didn't really feel.

Others, upon losing a toxic partner, responded in the exact opposite way. This was unexpected to me and something I read about, and then observed, in an acquaintance who lost her husband.

My friend "Janet" (fake name with details changed for obvious reasons) had a husband who had issues with alcohol and was abusive when he was alive. She had tried to leave him numerous times but found it difficult because he was manipulative and controlling. However, after he died in a car accident that he himself caused because of drunk driving, she completely re-imagined him as a perfect husband.

I remember the first time I realized she was doing this. I was over at her house having a cup of coffee and she started crying. "I just miss him so much. He was so good. Too good for this world. It's always the best who die young."

I didn't know how to respond. First of all, he was in his 70s. Second, the last time I had seen her, shortly before his death, she had only spoken about him in four-letter words. It had actually been uncomfortable how angry she had been and knowing that she wasn't choosing to leave, but that's how people get trapped in cycles of abuse and why it can be so devastating watching them go through the same patterns over and over again. And then suddenly, this. I assumed it was just the shock of grief talking. Surely, she didn't actually think that?

But she never spoke badly of him again that I heard. Suddenly, the man who had beaten her and drank himself insensible almost every night became a saint in her eyes. She started spending enormous amounts of time decorating and creating altars to him that sat right beside her front door so you couldn't miss it when you visited her.

Janet would place his photograph centrally in the place of honor almost like you would a guru or god. She would then light a candle beneath it every morning and then place a tiny shot glass of rum, his favorite drink, there every night.

Perhaps she felt guilty. I don't know. They say you never can truly know what goes on in others' relationships. However, in some books and online forums other people have talked about this experience as well. The need to suddenly "make things right" post-mortem or wanting to re-create a simple, easier version of their spouse or relationship, for a range of complex reasons that all boil down to somehow wanting to lessen suffering.

## FORGETTING

I felt guilty too, because despite all my efforts, I realized that I was increasingly beginning to forget Marcelo and others were even noticing. For example, at the first Christmas after his death. It was only a couple of months. Not even that long. How could I?

At that point, I was experiencing all those headaches, toothaches and throat pain, so looking back I can understand why that might have happened. Some days I could barely get out of bed, but at the time I felt so very ashamed. As if I was failing at grief.

My daughter mentioned, in passing, a dessert Marcelo had always loved to eat on Christmas Day and casually asked if I had made it. I had completely forgotten about it. If he had been alive, it would have been unthinkable not to make it but now that he was no longer here with me, it didn't even cross my mind. Not once.

Marcelo had always had a bit of a sweet tooth. Where we grew up, around Christmas time, aside from eating the Italian fruit bread panettone it is also quite common to make a type of peanut brittle called Garrapiñadas.

Marcelo used to love that and munch on it throughout the holiday season. Once upon a time, earlier in our relationship, I used to nag him to stop but eventually gave it up as a lost cause. Marcelo had his own mind and loved the stuff so much. It was one of his only real vices so I used to give in and stock up on tins of the stuff in advance, for his holiday binge.

None of the rest of us liked it that much, but as soon as I would see it or smell it, I would think of him. So, when I even forgot to consider it that first Christmas, I felt embarrassed. It just became so clear that meeting his needs was no longer my first priority, as it had been for the past couple of years when he was ill.

Forgetting peanut brittle isn't so serious, but after that I began to forget other things. Things I thought I could never forget. Such as exactly how low his voice was and how fast he talked. I couldn't remember if we talked in Spanish or English about certain things anymore.

Since we grew up in Argentina and then lived in the US as adults, there were very specific parts of our lives when we only talked to each other in one language versus the other. Finally, I began to forget his smell. First, I forgot how he smelled when he was ill. Then I forgot how he smelled when he was healthy. It was watching Janet and her altar that helped me forgive myself.

I realized that I couldn't do what she was doing and would have to remember him as best I could. I made sure to share as many stories as I could with our kids and asked them to do the same in return. Instead of trying to be the keeper of his torch, I asked others, who were better at keeping those types of details in their memory, to remind me sometimes of things I didn't want to forget. And then, eventually, I accepted that I would also just forget parts of him as well.

Partially because that's what I do. And, partially, because that's a natural part of the bereavement process and letting go.

---

When we lose a spouse, we all have to learn how to interact with the ghosts they leave behind but also to give them some distance, by allowing ourselves to begin to forget the small things eventually, which gives our hearts a break from holding them too close.

# 5

# THE QUEST: WANTING ANSWERS

Most of us want a life that makes sense. Where there are answers for our questions. But death often refuses to give those to us and so, part of grief is seeking answers in a void. Understanding, finally, that we may never get all the answers that have become so desperately important to our well-being is part of what happens when we finally begin to accept death and stop grieving.

Sometimes, our most important questions are around why someone died. Why was it them and not someone else? Or, why did they die the way they did? Or, could it have been avoided? The saddest and hardest question that we who are grieving ask ourselves, though, is if we could have done something differently.

WHAT IF?

I know this question well. I wondered at some points if we could have saved Marcelo if he had gone to see a doctor more regularly, or earlier. Maybe I should have insisted he go to annual appointments. Perhaps I should have made him go to the doctor to get blood tests as soon as he started complaining of feeling unwell.

Of course, everything looks different in retrospect. It is so easy to be wise and see what we should and could have done. At the time, of course, it didn't seem so serious. It didn't seem necessary. He didn't seem that ill.

Marcelo was just always so healthy. At least, it appeared that way. Now, I know that wasn't true. But for years he was my Tarzan. None of us ever thought that he would be the one to get cancer. We just wouldn't have believed it if someone had told us to guess which one in the family would get cancer. None of us would have said Marcelo.

But what if we hadn't had those blinders on? What if, what if, what if? Eventually, I stopped wondering. I knew that it wasn't helping me and certainly wasn't helping him.

The main question I have now is if I could have stopped some of the physical suffering he went through. I know

I did the best I could with the knowledge I had at the time. Even so, I later learned a number of techniques that I wish I had known when he was hurting. Things that now help me lessen the amount of physical pain I experience.

After all those unnecessary root canals, I eventually came across Dr. Joe Dispenza. If you have never heard of him, he writes books and creates videos to help people deal with pain. After being hit by a car while bicycling in a triathlon, Joe broke numerous vertebrae in his back and ended up experiencing ongoing pain. He then used meditation and visualization, instead of the surgery a wide range of doctors told him he would need, to heal his body and his pain.

I didn't know about those techniques or Dr. Joe Dispenza when Marcelo was dying, but they have since helped me and I believe they would have been incredibly beneficial for Marcelo as well. And so, part of me sometimes feels guilty, when I learn things that I can see might have "saved" Marcelo retrospectively from having suffered as much as he did.

I certainly didn't have those techniques at the time (or wouldn't have put myself through all those root canals after he died), but still question why I didn't. Why did he have to suffer? I suppose there is a part of me that fears maybe I wasn't trying to save him hard enough.

Or else, maybe I would have found some of these answers sooner.

And, maybe the tiny child inside of me is still asking if that's why he died? Because I just wasn't able to be a superhero with all sorts of invisible powers who could take away all his pain. And I couldn't find a way to keep him alive. Why couldn't my love protect him from dying or, at least, feeling so much pain?

## WHY, GOD?

Even if you don't believe in God, I think that part of the grief process involves a "Why, God?" stage. Why did s/he have to die? Was there a reason for it? Perhaps things do happen for a reason. In a strange way, looking back, I can also accept that cancer did actually improve Marcelo's and our family's quality of life in some ways. This feels like a horrible sentence to think, and an even darker one to write, as cancer is what took him away from us and eventually killed Marcelo.

Nevertheless, it remains at least a partial truth in the back of my mind. Obviously, it would have been better if he, and we, could have learned what he did from his experiences with cancer while also conquering it and remaining alive. But it is still important to point out that cancer did not have a purely negative impact on Marcelo and our lives.

When Marcelo was diagnosed, he was a company director with plenty of responsibilities and in charge of many people. He was busy, stressed and obsessed with efficiency. After getting his diagnosis, he was signed off and never returned to work in the eight years until his death.

That change was sudden and a difficult transition for him but, in the end, he accepted that there is more to life than efficiency. That patience can be a virtue. He became much more tolerant and compassionate with people who cannot move or work as fast, work as hard, exercise as much or eat as healthily as he did. It was a hard way for him to have to learn all that, but when he died, he was much more "chill" about other people and life. He wasn't a bad person before he got ill by any means, but by the time he died he had undeniably evolved personally and spiritually on many levels. It was evident to everyone he interacted with. He had changed.

He just had gained a completely new perspective about what is important and had learned not to react to other people's drama as much. His last eight years were very tough, for him as well as for us beyond just his physical illness, but a bonding was able to emerge between us all that was not there when life was much faster because we were all healthy.

For that reason, I credit Bill, Marcelo's bone marrow donor, for giving us the best eight years of our lives. Definitely not the most fun, but the ones with the most growth. When Marcelo was diagnosed he was stressed about potentially leaving me with a big mortgage on the house and two kids still navigating high school.

When he finally left us, we had paid off most of the house and both kids had college degrees. They both went on to do postgraduate degrees as well. They grew into well-educated and well-adjusted adults despite what they grew up with, and we were both very proud of how they dealt with his dying. I still am.

I believe he died in peace. I think he was ready to die and let go because all those things he was worried about when he was first diagnosed had been sorted out. At least in my mind, that's how I've answered those questions I had.

Now, when I ask myself why he died, I tell myself that I think he learned what he came to this Earth to learn. As I mentioned before, I think that our bodies are just housing our souls. Once our souls have learned what they need to learn, and done what they need to do, then they leave. Marcelo had learned what he needed to learn, and done what he needed to do. Maybe, if you put it another way, he'd taught us what we needed to learn as well.

## REDIRECTING YOUR QUESTIONS

When someone dies, most people feel some guilt about something. Many seem to examine their relationships and their spouse's death with a fine-toothed comb to see where they went wrong. That type of examination is a way of trying to find a sense of control in their life again. Even if it doesn't make sense from the outside.

Underneath the relentless questioning, is often something along the lines of, "Maybe it's all my fault! And maybe it's better to be 'bad,' and guilty, than feeling completely lost and powerless as I do right now."

Sometimes, of course, the surviving spouse didn't try their best and was to blame in significant ways for the suffering or even death of their partner. But that is not the situation I'm talking about here. Unfortunately, those types of people don't usually reflect on their relationships in my experience.

Rather, it's the ones who truly loved their partners who go through phases of feeling guilt, anger, confusion and then being lost because they are deeply examining their role in the relationship that was. And none of us are ever perfect, of course.

The sad truth is that we can't bring their spouse back to life or make things better anymore because we're the only ones left. Eventually, most realize that instead of continuously looking back at our old relationships, we need to focus on who is around us, alive and available now.

For this reason, many therapists and grief counselors recommend talking to your dead spouse as a way of dealing with their death. That doesn't necessarily mean believing that they are present with you or can hear you, but it helps you acknowledge their importance in your life. The main issue to pay attention to when doing this to ensure that you are not trying to get them to return "back" to you.

When Marcelo's presence appeared in my life, I found it comforting but didn't feel the need to hang on to him. Again, when people begin talking to their dead spouses as intended, in a healthy manner, it's so that you are able to create a "space" in your life for them, but not so that they remain the focus of your life.

In one, you are acknowledging your love while still allowing your life to continue with others who are living around you. The other approach would be to try to bridge that distance in ways that can be detrimental, where the focus would continue to be only on communicating with the dead spouse and not allowing for life around you to come back in.

I mentioned earlier that I have had numerous, ongoing experiences of feeling Marcelo's presence. For me, I believe it actually is his ghost, I suppose. Others would only think they are speaking to a version they have created of their dead spouse in their mind. However, although the sense of Marcelo actually being there in the room with me faded over time, and he began to feel more like a ghost the longer he was dead, it reassured me that I hadn't "lost" him even if I was forgetting details about him and our life together.

While that was a sad process, I realize now that it was also necessary for me to let him go. Forgetting small parts of him meant that he was not always so close to me anymore and allowed me mental and emotional space to let new people in. It meant that since I could not arm myself with the ghost of his memories anymore, others were able to get through the chinks of his memories.

I hadn't consciously meant to be holding others at arm's length with memories of him, but that was their ultimate effect. Part of the reason I had wanted to hold on to those details about him so badly was that I wanted to keep his memory alive for our children, like I said. But perhaps I was also subconsciously waiting for him to keep appearing back in my life, without actually realizing it, and so keeping others out.

I didn't initially speak to Ivan and Sabina about my experiences of feeling his presence when they happened. I'm not sure why. I wasn't worried that they wouldn't understand. Maybe I had just wanted to keep it private until I knew he seemed to be keeping coming back and staying around.

When I finally mentioned it, Sabina gasped loudly and clapped her hands. "Oh my God Mom, I knew it! I feel him too. Like regularly."

"What? How? When?"

"Well, he knows better than to bother me when I have a knife in my hand," she laughed. Then got a sad smile on her face. "Remember 'La Misa Criolla'?"

During the long hours by his bedside in the last few days of his life, the kids prepared a playlist of his favorite songs for him, even though they weren't sure he would hear or recognize them anymore.

Marcelo had always loved music and especially connected with my daughter through music, by exchanging songs they thought the other would like.

For them, sending each other a new song was code for, "I love you and I'm thinking of you."

In that playlist that the kids prepared was a song that was particularly meaningful to him, "La Misa Criolla." Even I don't know all the reasons it meant so much to Marcelo. It is interesting how you can live with someone, and love them almost their entire life, and they can still have their secrets and parts of their lives you know so little about. Not in a bad way, it's just that they are a part of your life but also separate.

"La Misa Criolla" was a song that had marked several key events in his life and he loved it with a passion I never quite understood. But we all knew he adored that song so, of course, the kids put it in his playlist.

I had read somewhere that hearing, and the ability to relate to musical memory in particular, is the last sense to go, so we were all by his bedside chatting with each other but not expecting Marcelo to be able to relate to us or the world anymore, as song by song played in the background.

However, when "La Misa Criolla" popped up, Marcelo's facial expression changed significantly. We all noticed it. He went from being slack-faced and expressionless to having a far-away, half smile. I called it his "Mona Lisa face." It was the same expression I recognized when his mother walked through the door. She didn't even speak or touch him. As soon as she came into the room, he knew and gave that same smile.

So, we all knew that, even in his last moments, Marcelo responded deeply to music. And Sabina felt that after he died, he continued to communicate with her through music the way they always had, to continue to say, "I love you and I'm thinking of you."

She would often hear music playing, a song they had shared suddenly wafting in unexpectedly when she was thinking of him or needed encouragement. Another example is that whenever she gets into an Uber, the first song that is playing on the radio station is usually one that has meaning to them.

This feels significant to her because he used to complain about having to be her "taxi driver" when she was growing up and needed someone to drive her places. When she wouldn't ask him nicely for a lift, he would always respond with, "What am I, your taxi driver?" She would make it up to him in the car by playing some music that she knew he would like.

For us, as a family, these combined experiences of feeling Marcelo's presence after he was gone, helped us stop questioning what had happened to him and what happens after death. We don't know exactly, but for us as a family, because of these repeated experiences, it is clear that the soul somehow lives on.

---

When someone dies, especially a spouse, part of the grieving process is seeking answers about their life and death and the role you played in it.

# 6

# THE STAGES: TOWARDS ACCEPTANCE

I f you have read anything about grief, you have probably read about the five stages: denial, anger, bargaining, depression and acceptance. Much has been written about them, so I am not going to add to that here except to share about the point when I finally accepted my grief, and some of what my journey leading up to that looked like.

After Marcelo died, because some of our business interests had been tied together and he had helped me so much with my business, many of his emails started getting forwarded to me to make sure that I did not miss subscriptions or important notifications.

That meant that, every day after his death, I was receiving emails that said, "Hi Marcelo!" Email after email after email would clutter my inbox, reminding me that I now had to play his role because he was no longer alive.

Even worse, they would often start off with something such as, "Dear Marcelo, We are reaching out because we haven't heard from you in a while." Or "We have the perfect job opportunity for you Marcelo!"

These were all, of course, random mass emails that meant nothing for the people sending them but when I received them, they drilled a hole in my soul. I felt like angrily replying, "You have not heard from him because he is dead, you idiots." Or, "He does not need that job opportunity, or any opportunities for anything ever again actually, thanks for reminding me."

The worst was when I received communications from my condominium association addressed to him as the "Primary Owner," saying "Hello Marcelo, we hope you can join us tonight for the Homeowner's Meeting." These are people who were my neighbors and very clearly know I am a widow.

I could keep getting mad, but it reminds me that in some ways they never knew him, never cared that much and that the world keeps moving on no matter what happens or who dies, even though when I was grieving it felt to me like the world ended. And then, I shut off my computer, stuck my head out of my house and found that it hadn't. I was a little annoyed and angry to realize that to be honest.

I was so annoyed and angry with the world in general for allowing Marcelo to die, and then not grieving him enough along with me, that I decided I couldn't stay in New Jersey anymore.

I couldn't walk the same streets and see the people and try to pick up the old pieces of the life I had with Marcelo. I was ready to punch someone. So, I moved to Florida. Suddenly. With only our dog Apollo.

## WHEN IT RAINS, IT POURS

It has been proven that, during bereavement, you are not only more angry sometimes, you are also more physically vulnerable. There is actually something called "broken heart syndrome." The technical term for it is Takotsubo Syndrome. That is when someone develops serious heart problems after an unexpected loss or sudden illness.

In my life, that vulnerability showed up as an increasing amount of physical pain, accident and loss. The world just didn't care for me anymore. It had let Marcelo die, and then everyone I loved was getting hurt or injured as well.

For example, Marcelo's mother was staying with me in the last month before, and then for some time after, his death. Of course, she was distraught and not feeling quite like her normal self. She also had cancer as well. So, it wasn't a complete surprise, given all that and her age, that she slipped in the shower one month after Marcelo died and broke her back. It, literally, broke her.

It broke me too. It was the last straw. Everything was going wrong in New Jersey. It felt suffocating. I began to hate it there and wanted to escape. So, six months after his death, I left New Jersey where our family's life had been rooted. I found that there were just too many memories there. Everyone knew me as half of Marcelo and Sandra.

When they saw me alone, I knew they always saw Marcelo's absence. I wanted to find a place where I could learn to just be me. Where people wouldn't know to automatically look for him. I wanted to move to a place where he wasn't so close. Also, I wanted a place with sun. Marcelo had never really missed it when we moved to the US but I had. So while New Jersey had been good to us in many ways, it was too cold for me and if I was starting a new life, my new life was going to be warmer. And be beside the ocean.

I chose to move to Florida with my beloved German Shepherd dog, Apollo. He had been our dog. He was still a puppy, really. Maybe I transferred some of my discomfort to him when we left, but Apollo was never happy in Florida. He had a difficult time settling in and started to react to strangers (which was pretty much everyone because I was new there).

I lived in a condominium with strangers walking past all the time. Apollo needed behavioral help and the things I tried didn't work. It wasn't good for him, or for anyone else's peace of mind either.

At that point in my life, I decided that trying to re-train him was beyond me, so I sent him away to a dog trainer someone had recommended. He said that they would be able to help solve the issue in a week by boarding him at their kennel and doing intensive training there. I dropped him off but then got a call from them only a couple of hours later. I was worried that maybe he had bitten someone, but it was much worse than that.

The trainer said, "Apollo didn't make it."

I couldn't understand what he was telling me so, confusedly, I was prepared to go pick him up.

"Didn't make what? Has he failed the training already? Are you sending him home now? Do I have to come pick him up?"

"He's dead. I'm sorry. There was an accident."

Another death. More grieving I would have to process when I had come to Florida to get away from that.

I could keep on listing the things that happened to me but it's enough to say that once Marcelo died, and grief entered my life, it's as if it opened the floodgates to allow bad luck into the rest of my life as well, at least for a while.

You could see it from a different perspective as well, though: Life was telling me it was time to start completely afresh. That poor Apollo couldn't settle in Florida because he didn't belong there. And that I needed to not try to recreate my old life from New Jersey down in Florida. I needed to grieve and accept Marcelo's death, and then pick up the pieces of myself and my life and figure out what I could make with them.


PIECE BY PIECE

My Florida condominium had just a few pieces of furniture originally: a bed, a lamp, and a sofa. I had sent a few boxes by truck with personal items like books, clothes, and some trophies from the kids' swimming competitions. It was purposely bare in many ways so that I could start figuring out my new life and my new me, piece by piece.

Florida seemed the perfect place for it, since there are so many other people that go there to do the same thing: to retire and start new lives in the sun. And, I may be wrong, but this state seems to have more widows and widowers per capita than any other place I've ever visited, so my grieving seemed more normal here than in New Jersey.

Eventually, I slowly began to admit in public that I was a widow. Over and over again, people's eyes would become gentle, they would tear up faintly or their bodies would soften and I would understand that they too knew what I was going through.

When my boxes arrived, a few days after I moved to Florida, the delivery man had me sign some papers to verify their receipt. Since there was no table, we both sat on the sofa to review the paperwork.

While I was signing the papers, the tall, Haitian delivery guy looked slowly around at the bare space in the living room with no furniture and just some boxes, and Apollo the German Shepherd sleeping on the floor.

He asked me, "Are you going to live alone here? With nothing but these boxes and a dog?"

That is when it hit me and it hit me hard. Marcelo wasn't going to be following me down shortly and the kids now had their own lives. I was no longer part of a "we." I was a "me." I had never been or lived alone before.

I took a couple of deep breaths as I looked around at the boxes. The delivery guy had actually already gotten off the couch and was about to leave but when he saw I was starting to cry, instead of leaving, he sat back down.

That complete stranger, who never even told me his name, sat beside me while I cried non-stop while thinking about what I had just done: why had I decided to move to Florida? I didn't actually know anyone there. I had just left the only world I knew behind. It was at that exact moment that I realized the immensity of my decision. I had lived in my parents' house until I got married, for goodness' sake!

The delivery guy looked at me with deep compassion and said, "Sister, you need a hug."

And so he gave me a long, brotherly hug until I stopped crying, a long while later.

My emotions were so deep that six years later, I am crying as I write this and revisit that experience, wiping tears away in front of my computer. However, it was precisely what I needed. That hug marked the exact moment when I truly started my mourning and, eventually, my healing process.

The tiny amount of possessions I took down to Florida with me is a very good metaphor for how small our world and our focus often becomes after a spouse dies. Many people stop "living" and taking care of themselves and their lives the way they did before.

They stop eating healthily, keeping up with friends, going to church, doing the hobbies they once loved, and even tending the homes and possessions that were once their pride and joy. What's the point? All the external things that defined them can often fall away, until they become a shell of whom they once were.

That delivery guy will never know how significant his presence was in my life. That is the moment when I stopped having just lost Marcelo and started on my journey towards processing the pain of my loss. I wasn't ready before. I wasn't in the "right place" in all sorts of ways: physically, mentally, emotionally. But finally, in my empty new condo, having cleared out everything I had needed to get rid of from my old life, stuff that was holding me back, I finally had the space to let my tears fall and begin to tend my wounds. That's the day I truly started my journey with grief. So, thank you to that delivery man who unknowingly helped me on my journey back to life again.

Grief is so all-encompassing for many people that it literally shrinks them, and they often need someone else to show them how small their world has become through loss. The point at which they truly recognize its effects, is when they can truly begin to heal.

# 7

# THE QUESTION: NEW IDENTITY

A t this point in the book, I want to switch from mostly concentrating on telling stories about my grief over losing Marcelo, to sharing some tips and tools that help one progress through the mourning process and start to live again. For this reason, I will also start addressing you, the reader, as I want this to become more of a conversation.

One of the first steps of mourning is to find ways to externalize your grief. In whatever ways work for you. Many grief counselors, for example, recommend finding some small rituals to do regularly in the beginning, such as lighting a candle or buying your spouse's favorite flowers, and then slowly decreasing the frequency of that over time, as you begin to let go of your bereavement and begin to live again.

## MOURNING CLOTHES

One of the first steps in beginning to mourn, rather than just grieve, is to find ways to separate the feelings you have inside of you and turn them into rituals. A major part of the grief therapy process is developing ways to ritually acknowledge and remember a spouse at certain times and in specific ways, like I mentioned above.

The reason for doing this is that it means that you begin to control your grief narrative, rather than feeling as if the emotions are only, and always, in control of you. That's why, for example, wearing black is a stereotypical mourning rite.

Wearing black shows everyone that you are bereaved. That some light/life/color has been taken from your life for a period, and you need darkness to recover. It also allows and reminds you that you need to give yourself time to feel those darker emotions that, at other points in our lives, we would usually not advertise or allow ourselves to feel for long periods.

I didn't wear black continuously for those first couple of months, but I did notice myself feeling drawn to many similar things. Needing darkness. Needing to retreat. Needing to fall apart. At first it scared me; I thought I was depressed and not coping well and wanted to hide that, so initially struggled against it.

We are so scared of pain and being depressed in our society nowadays that I wanted to get rid of it right away, and ended up not truly allowing myself to grieve until I felt safe in Florida, surrounded by sunshine.

It was only there, when I finally felt comforted by the presence of so much sun and light, that I felt it would be safe to begin experiencing the full darkness of my grief. That is when I finally gave myself permission to fall apart after the delivery guy hugged me. To cry for as long as I needed.

Many cultures have specific traditions that allow the grieving space and time to cry. It also gives them rituals and marks them out specifically so that everyone else knows what they are doing. In some cultures, they cover themselves with ashes or mud. In Victorian England, widows were expected to wear black, and remain in mourning, for two years as that is how long they thought it took someone to get over a spouse.

In China and across Asia, they traditionally wear white while mourning and the period for a spouse is one year. That amount of time is similar for Catholics, who are still sometimes formally advised to mourn a spouse for a year and a day, with one month of "heavy mourning" initially.

If you are grieving someone or even something, have you tried any rituals to help you mourn? Rituals that mark you out as grieving can help. Do you think that actually wearing black, purposely retreating, or something similar, could help your process in some way?

Maybe it would feel counter-intuitive or morbid at first, as if you should be focused on "getting better," but actually it seems that those who try to bypass grief struggle the most in the long term. Finding ways to mark yourself as grieving helps remind you that the feelings and the sudden changes in your emotions are not "crazy" but related to your loss. It also helps remind friends and loved ones of your loss as well.

I've heard some people talk about purposely wearing black, and it makes sense to me now even though at the time, I didn't want to be seen as depressed or depressing. I wanted to be seen as coping well and functioning. But I now recognize that by doing that, I didn't give myself permission to grieve the way I needed to. I had to wait until Florida where I felt safe in the sun.

I look back now and wonder if that is why I ended up experiencing all those headaches and needing those root canals. Because I didn't give in to the sadness and pain in my heart, my body expressed it for me. There are simply some things we cannot repress, no matter how much we do not want to have to experience them. I did not want Marcelo to be dead and did not want to be grieving him. But my body knew I was in pain anyway and it kept telling me that I was sad, even when I was trying not to feel it. At first, I refused to listen and tried to get doctors and dentists to take it away. Eventually, I listened and my phantom pain disappeared.

For many others, they do not have issues feeling sad, they just do not want to talk about their private feelings with others. Your clothes can be a physical indicator as to how you are progressing in your bereavement, both to yourself and others. It can be a way for those who love and are close to you to more easily "read" how you are feeling without constantly having to ask.

Are you feeling completely lost and despairing today? Great, on go the jet-black earrings, plus the black patterned scarf with beaded fringe and those gothic booties on top of a completely black outfit. If you feel a tiny glimmer of hope then maybe a small, silver accessory. If you're feeling almost optimistic, then perhaps a pink bag so you can take it off and hide it if your mood changes.

The thing about wearing all black, when you've lost someone you love, is that it announces to everyone what has just happened, especially if they know that you're doing this on purpose. That you once had a partner, and now you do not and you are sad and need to be treated carefully, and expectations of you adjusted because of that fact.

The useful thing about dressing this way is it can be a response to all those questions about your emotions. When people ask you how you are doing, instead of telling them, which can be a very difficult conversation and feel invasive, you can deflect the question and tell them you've decided to "dress your feelings" for the next couple of months. And then let them figure it out from there.

If you don't want to be constantly asked anymore how you're feeling, you could even start telling people that when you're starting to feel better or having a good day, you'll start wearing color so it will be obvious, but would prefer if they'd stop asking or commenting on it as this is going to be a long and complex journey for you, and you hope they can respect that.

And, of course, you don't have to wear black. You can put (and light) a black candle in your window every night. You could wear black jewelry. You could get a tattoo in commemoration. There are many time-honored traditions that may feel more appropriate to you.

## SHARING GRIEF

What mourning rites usually do initially is to separate the bereaved from the rest of the community while they come to terms with their loss. Since grief and bereavement aren't as well understood in many cultures anymore, you may not have known to prepare for the way it takes over your life and tears you apart. However, there are many others around you who are experiencing, or have experienced, grief as well.

It may help to find ways to connect with those around you who have experienced similar loss. If you do not want to do it in person via local support groups, friends or family, there are an increasing number of podcasts being produced where widow(er)s talk about their deeply personal experiences with grief.

Many podcasts also interview or coach others, asking them to share the thoughts and emotions that they wouldn't even tell their best friends, so you get to hear a wide range of views and experiences. If you Google "widow grief podcast," or similar keywords, you will come up with links to the latest podcasts on this topic and I highly recommend listening to some.

If podcasts are not for you, there are certainly many Facebook groups, websites and online support groups where you can listen and discuss your experiences with others as widow(er)s. If you Google "widow grief support groups," you will find numerous links of the most active in your area.

Engaging in these types of groups not only reassured me that I was not the only one to experience the emotions and ups and downs that I had, it also prepared me for understanding that I was now a widow. And, also, now part of a community of loss and widows and widowers around the world who understood. Although going through that loss was incredibly lonely, I wasn't alone in that experience.

## TELLING PEOPLE YOU ARE A WIDOW/WIDOWER

While I was grieving, I hadn't even thought much about the fact I had become a widow. Listening to others' stories helped me realize I wasn't alone. But in fact, the first time I realized I myself was an actual widow was when I went back to Argentina. I mentioned before that my mother-in-law had broken her back shortly after Marcelo died. She stayed with me recuperating for another month or so, but eventually needed to go back to Argentina for more long-term, ongoing treatment.

I flew back with her. Since I was there, I decided to renew my Argentine passport and went to my appointment where the Officer went through all their normal series of questions to fill in the form. Name, age… all those types of things.

Finally, she asked, "What is your civil status?" I didn't respond.

She asked me again, "What is your civil status?" I didn't respond again.

She looked at me, a little annoyed at this point and questioned, "Are you single, married, divorced, or a widow?"

Finally, after a long pause, I whispered, "Widow." And then immediately started crying.

That was the first time I had to say it out loud. "I'm a widow." It felt awful to vocalize the word "widow" about myself, which is why I started crying in the passport office. The officer stopped filling out the form and came to my side of the desk and hugged me.

"I understand," she said. "I'm so sorry it's happened to you, too."

My suggestion now, looking back, is to prepare for emerging as a widow very purposefully rather than having it catch you unawares like it did me. Of course, in those first couple of months, everything is a haze and you need to retreat and cocoon yourself in grief for a while.

However, during the initial grief period, you restrict your interactions with the outside world, and everything about your life is somehow focused on death and mourning, so if people ask about your spouse or death it does not catch you unawares because it is all you think about.

But then, there will come a time when you leave that constant focus on death behind. When that happens, then you need to prepare for people to bring up your spouse or death in passing. People who do not know that he or she has died, who ask you if you ever married or what your marital status is.

These are very simple everyday situations where you need to explain that you are a widow or widower. If you have not figured out what to say, then every time it comes up it could potentially be another minor shock. Over and over again.

My suggestion is to practice writing it down as a sentence a couple of times, saying it to yourself in the mirror and then to a trusted friend or someone close when you are beginning to emerge again into the world, "I have lost my partner. My spouse died recently. I am a widow(er)."

I would recommend finding a way to practice that. Some more extroverted types would probably do that with a family member or friend. Others might just repeat the lines a couple of times to themselves. Regardless, you just need to have an idea of what you want to say so that when the topic comes up with a stranger, or someone who doesn't know your spouse has died, it doesn't catch you unprepared in the moment.

Often, our grief can become controlled by how others view us or by overwhelming emotions. But you can begin to take control of your grief, and your narrative around it, by consciously and purposefully mourning.

# 8

# THE NAVIGATING: LONG-TERM GRIEF

I n the last chapter, I began to talk about ways to externalize your grief that could help you begin to come to terms with your new status as "griever" and widow(er).

In this chapter, I want to talk about some things that can potentially help deal with long-term grief. Many people only think about dealing with grief or mourning during the bereavement period. Many expect that sadness and the sense of loss will come to an end once your official bereavement ends.

However, unfortunately, for most of us that is not the case. Grief is something that keeps returning over and over again. That is why you need to prepare to deal with it in the long term as well. In this chapter, I will just talk about coping with the ongoing presence of grief in your life. In later chapters, I will talk about new relationships and other aspects related to this topic.

When something uncomfortable and unwanted is in your life, it can cause you suffering. Eventually though, ideally, you find ways to deal with it so that it is no longer as painful or problematic. This chapter will look at a range of ways that people have adapted to grief in the long term and some techniques they've learned to distance themselves from it. The coping strategies I mention do not get rid of the grief, but they do help reduce its impact on your life.

## CONTROLLING PAIN

When I started listening and engaging with Dr. Joe Dispenza's work, he changed my perspective on a lot of things. Not just how I dealt with pain, but how I focused my energy. One of Joe's common themes is that we come to this Earth to experience pain. So, although many of his techniques help to successfully alleviate it, he does not see that as the main goal.

Looking back, I see that one of the reasons Marcelo's illness, and then my grief, shrank my world so much is that it didn't leave me with time or energy for anything else. It also meant that I often couldn't look forwards or even backwards, either. We, and then I, were just often stuck in a horrible present suffering and pain and loss.

Ironically, one of the reasons that Marcelo's life got better in some ways towards the end is that his focus decreased so dramatically. He stopped worrying about everything that was to come, or that could happen, and that meant he was able to just be in the present more. Which, ultimately, often made him much happier.

This is what the concept of mindfulness is about. Instead of trying to be happy all the time, or forcing your experiences into what you think they should be, it focuses on accepting whatever emotions and reality you find yourself having. Instead of trying to push the emotions away for those you would prefer (or have lost), you examine and deal with those in your present.

Joe also suggests doing the opposite. Confusing? I hope this will make sense within the next couple of paragraphs. Mindfulness helps you accept "what is" in your life so that you suffer less when you are faced with bad things you cannot change. Joe Dispenza's techniques help you create more of what you want when you are in situations that you *do* have the power to change.

When you're being buffeted by wave after wave of loss and pain though, it can become so overwhelming that you drown in negativity. Joe taught me to start visualizing a better focus for myself and my life. With his method, you start thinking beyond and around the pain. Do you see the difference?

We can't control everything in our lives, but we can control how we react to things. We can often control how much pain we feel and suffering we have, in response to negative situations in particular. Therefore, instead of only trying to heal or stop suffering, you focus beyond the pain with Joe's approach. I started asking myself questions, and visualizing, things such as, "What might my life look like if I was happy and thriving even with Marcelo gone?"

Joe recommends focusing your energy on creating a positive reality. This is, in many ways, like the Law of Attraction and other popular concepts like manifestation. With many of these ideas, you practice something over and over again in your imagination until you can "see it" and believe it as a possible reality. Many religions, even magic, build upon this technique as a way of transforming negative situations into something better.

While I found Joe's work on visualizing desired outcomes to be especially helpful, there are many different religious, spiritual traditions and transformative processes that can help you shift your focus from suffering to empowerment. If you want to try something like this, you just need something that suits your personality and belief system; even prayer can do something similar if that feels more appropriate to you.

## CREATING CALM SPACES

Once you have experienced deep trauma, many different types of research have shown that the emotions actually lodge in your body, so you often need to do more than just visualization and prayer. In fact, an early book on the topic of grieving childhood trauma by Babette Rothschild was called *The Body Remembers* (2000).

In that book, she explored the concept of "somatic memory" and how certain traumatic experiences and emotions are stored in particular places in the body that they are somehow connected with.

For example, when I had all that tooth pain after Marcelo died, you could explain it away by saying that I might have just begun grinding and clenching my teeth at night (bruxism). That is a very common response to deep stress and trauma. When it happens over time, your jaw muscles begin to freeze up and many people develop long-term issues with headaches, migraines and neck problems like I did.

However, Rothschild's approach would look at the fact that I was experiencing pain in my head, mouth and

116 | SANDRA CAMPONOGARA

throat, initially, a little differently. She would probably suggest that there was something significant about it being connected to the place that we usually produce thoughts and words. That maybe there was something I was repressing, hadn't said or needed to express.

If so, she was right. At that point, I was trying very hard to continue to function and still "be there" for everyone. Marcelo's mother, especially, needed attention because she was staying with me, had cancer and had broken her back. I also simply didn't want to grieve. After eight years of Marcelo dying, I wanted my bereavement to be over. So, initially, I tried to skip my grieving process and attempted to jump right back into my life after a couple of weeks.

At first, I seemed to be doing just fine. Everyone commented on how well I was coping. In some ways, I certainly was doing a lot better than even I had expected. But, in others, I knew I wasn't okay. Not at all, and I wasn't sure what to do about it. That's when my body stopped me and forced me to grieve. It gave me the space I needed.

However, by forcing me to stop in such an extreme manner, it now means that I have traumatic memories lodged in my neck, jaw and head and am now more susceptible whenever I experience stress. That's part of what I've had to accept about long-term grief.

In some ways, I'm wiser and more resilient now. But, I also need to take care of myself more than I did before Marcelo's illness and death. I can get physically over-whelmed and fall back into somatic pain and loss patterns that are now stored in my body, if I don't take care of myself and purposely relax.

Everyone I know that has experienced something similar—and become more vulnerable in this way—has ultimately had to develop a set of different tools based on their personal preference, if they don't want to lose their lives to chronic pain.

One friend has always been very sensual and loves food and smells. For that reason, she counteracts those somatic pain patterns by nurturing them with certain types of herbal teas, foods, and aromatherapy oils that she only uses when she knows she has been triggered and might be heading for another grief episode.

She found that always taking some roll-on travel bottles of key essential oils helps her create a calm space, wherever she may be, if she experiences a wave of grief unexpectedly when she is away from home. You can Google "essential oils for grief" to find many arti-cles and lists on the topic, but her favorite ones are lavender, sandalwood, geranium, and vetiver.

She also drinks saffron or chamomile tea and finds that they are very soothing when re-experiencing a deep sense of loss. As almonds have also always had positive associations for her, she also keeps a little baggy of them in her purse to munch on in a "grief emergency."

If she is going through a really difficult period, she digs into her special stash of marzipan that she buys on her holidays in Spain. It reminds her of times when she, and her body, was happy, relaxed and calm. So, she finds that eating tiny pieces of that with some coffee helps her body remember what that feels like.

Since my friend is so in touch with her body and emotions—she is my yoga teacher—she starts doing these things as soon as she notices her triggers begin-ning to act up, instead of waiting until she is having a full-blown grief episode. This means that any grief she needs to process can then be experienced but not be quite so overwhelming anymore, because she has found a way to distance herself from it.

Once you've been "around" grief long enough, it helps if you learn to recognize your physical signs that grief has been triggered, and develop some coping strategies for them. Those signs are different for everyone. Some people will start getting annoyed and itchy, others will start coughing. I get sleepy. Likewise, the things that you will find soothing, that help give you a tiny bit of distance while you experience your grief, will be different for you than for me or my friend.

Usually, what will work for you will be related to the things you like best or already have positive associations with. This is because, just like our body stores traumatic memories, it also stores positive memories as well. This means that you can shortcut your way back to happiness if you love Christmas by purposely smelling some "Christmas smells" at other times of the year.

Be creative and adapt this to your life. If you are someone who likes music, like Marcelo, then perhaps a grief playlist would be a good idea. If you respond well to movement, then perhaps a series of yoga poses. If you like art, then carry a sketchbook or some watercolors you can do briefly if your triggers arise.

The key is that you need to understand that once grief has lodged itself in your body, it likely will keep returning, and often will catch you unawares during inconvenient moments. Once you accept this, learn to recognize your triggers and have some (portable) coping techniques, then this no longer becomes something you have to fear or repress.

## MOVING

Increasing amounts of trauma research, starting with the Babette Rothschild book I mentioned from over twenty years ago, and more research and articles since, have shown that when people experience severe trauma or loss, their bodies remember. In order to help process their grief as effectively as possible, they need to move in some way and let the emotions and experience release from their bodies.

Movement has been one of the main ways I have used to help me deal with long-term grief. When I realized that I had gotten stuck and was not processing Marcelo's death in New Jersey, I literally moved. To Florida. That might sound extreme to some, but many others find that travel of some sort, even a brief holiday, where they literally move location, helps.

Part of it may be that no one in the new location knows you are grieving. Part of it may be that your brain has so many new things to focus on that it forgets to suffer. Or, maybe there is just something about traveling and actually moving from one place to another that can be healing as well.

There are many theories that certain locations and spaces, not only bodies, can hold energy. So, if you experienced trauma in one location, leaving it to go to a place where you were previously happy or have never been before could help relieve you of some of the "spiritual heaviness" that might still reside around you.

Just as I mentioned that I connected Marcelo's spirit somehow to our house in New Jersey, many others have made this type of connection in their own experiences as well. It makes sense then, even though you will still bring your grief with you, that traveling away from where you experienced a loss can help—literally as well as metaphorically—give you some distance from it.

Most though, when they talk about healing trauma through movement, actually mean various forms of exercise. Some run. Some do trauma-informed yoga. Some get gentle massages as they feel nurtured in a way their bodies often miss when losing a partner.

There are many ways you can use the body and movement to help release grief, and the appropriate technique or modality is really up to you. For me, after moving to Florida, I began to dance my grief away and that is something I will explain more in detail in the next couple of chapters.

At some point, when grieving a much-loved spouse, you will have to adjust yourself and your life in order to accommodate their absence. Most people who experience grief find ways to cope, but the pain never completely goes away. Eventually, most begin to develop a series of conscious coping techniques to help support them when their grief arises again. In this way, it no longer impacts and arrests their life as it did initially, and this is what I would recommend you do as well.

# 9

# THE NEED: LEARNING TO SAVE YOURSELF

A t some point, you will begin to emerge from your grief. I promise you that unless something is specifically blocking you and keeping you stuck, this is the trajectory that everyone naturally follows sooner or later. I know it doesn't feel that way at first. Believe me, I know.

Eventually though, somehow you begin to recognize that your sadness is at risk of consuming you. And then something inside you will begin to shout and kick and try to wake you up—by whatever means necessary (even sometimes using pain as it did with me)—so that you're forced to stop crying and learn to live again.

The way you will try to save yourself, however, may not look completely normal to those around you. In fact, it could look a little crazy at first, to others. Even to your-self. Many people who are grieving often find that when they try to stop grieving, it is their loved ones who are most judgmental of their efforts. Possibly they do this with the best of intentions, but I am not completely sure this is the case. Perhaps somewhere inside, your loved ones believe that you being sad somehow releases them of the need to grieve them-selves. And so they worry that if you stop crying, their tears will begin, so sometimes they sabotage your efforts to get well.

Whatever the reason, their lack of support can be unex-pected. Moreover, the things that normally help people relax—like a bubble bath or glass of wine—may simply not be enough anymore to help you find a way out of grief. I think it is because your nervous system is over-whelmed and needs something specifically and wonderfully (weirdly?) tailored to your needs to soothe it.

Others may be offering lots of suggestions, and most are well-intentioned, but there usually comes a time during grief where that can become oppressive and you need to take ownership of your healing and begin to chart your own path to wellness.

## WATCHING THE WAVES

For me, as I've already mentioned, it was around the six-month period that I began to realize that I wasn't really taking care of myself or even grieving properly after Marcelo died. I was stuck and felt I needed to do something extreme to help get myself back onto a path of wellness where I could begin to heal again.

I've always loved swimming. It's how I met Marcelo. But even before then, I was always a water baby. Swimming even before I could walk. I love floating in the sea. Being buffeted by the waves. The blues and greens and grays of the ocean. The salt in the air. Even the fog. Being near the seaside soothes me like nothing else.

I also like just walking on the beach. Burying my toes in the sand. Picking up warm, smooth pebbles and throwing them towards the boats while dogs frolic and bark in the distance. I watch them sail through the air until I hear satisfying plops in the froth.

I often take a book with me, that I never read, because I always end up just staring into the horizon. Smiling at the waves. Listening to the call of the sea. Looking for mermaids.

Like I said, I have always loved the ocean. When my body began to fall apart, and the root canals didn't work to take away my pain, I was lost. I didn't know what to do or where to go for help. So, I went to the one place I have always felt safe. I went to the ocean and She healed me.

To other people, it probably seemed like a crazy decision. There were times my choice didn't make sense to me either. Why had that mad, raving grief inside of me forced me down towards the Florida sun where I first got my headaches in the first place? It made absolutely no sense. If I was in my right mind, I would have run the other way.

Looking back now though, I can see that it was exactly what I needed. There was a deep, intuitive wisdom to that choice I made that I couldn't have explained at the time. Nonetheless, my sorrow forced me to go directly to the only place that would completely break me open, and experience the pain I needed to feel in order to survive.

I had just spent eight years previous to that trying very hard to help keep Marcelo alive. To attend to his every need. To be brave and courageous for him and our children and everyone else I loved in our life. Of course I didn't mind, it was exactly where I had wanted to be and what I had wanted to do. I was proud that we navigated those years together the way we did.

But then, I was left alone. Bereft and alone. And I needed to do something else. So, I did. It might have looked crazy to other people. In fact, I know it did. But perhaps that is the "gift" grief gives us. It stops us from caring so much about what others think. It allows us to do things we would never otherwise contemplate in our normal day-to-day existence.

I would encourage you, if you are still in the midst of grieving, to think about whether you are still trying to be polite and "holding up appearances" for others to the detriment of yourself. Are you in terrible pain? If so, that might be your body screaming at you to save yourself? Try to listen to it and figure out what it is telling you.

Sometimes you will find clues in where the pain is occurring in your body, or when it first started happening, or who was with you, or what it stopped you from doing. Instead of trying to carry on with your life through the pain, I would suggest that your body and the pain are trying to help you and telling you that you really need to start taking care of yourself. If this is true, you will often find that your body will escalate the pain every time you succeed in healing it by continuing to shut down your ability to go on with your life as normal.

I initially, will begin slowly with bouts of pain here and there. If you do not listen, and start grieving and taking care of yourself the way you need to, then it will start "shouting" at you and cause some sort of extreme pain that ensures you have to take care of yourself (and likely will not function normally again until you do).

The solutions you require to support your grieving and path to wellness may not be as extreme as mine, but are often connected to things you have loved for a long time. Things that made you feel good and free and soothed, even as a child, perhaps. How could you begin to remember what these once were, and somehow reconnect with them to support your well-being?

BREATHING LESSONS

One of the things I noticed when I moved to Florida and began spending more time at the beach, was how quickly my breathing changed. I recognized that my breathing had become anxious, quick and shallow in Marcelo's last years, for obvious reasons. My breathing was clearly reflecting my emotional state.

I mentioned noticing how my breathing had changed over coffee one day to my yoga teacher friend after a couple of months in Florida.

"That's not surprising," she responded. "In Ayurveda, and many other traditional medicinal approaches, they understand that the lungs are a place that holds grief. That's why so many people start smoking when they are sad or anxious."

"Really? I thought it was the waves that were helping me. I love listening to the waves at night. You think as I'm beginning to grieve less, my breathing is improving? That the two are connected?" I slurped my coffee in fascination.

She smiled. "That's part of it. There is a lot of research that shows listening to nature, like birdsong, the wind in the trees or waves, has a relaxing effect on the brain and body. Even if it is just through your headphones."

"Aaaah, it's not just in my mind!" I laughed.

"No, not at all." She smiled. "That's why so many spas and massage therapists have wave soundtracks. It actually helps their clients relax."

"For me, I need to be at the beach watching the waves as well though, for it to really work best when I'm upset. It gives my eyes and ears just enough to hear and see that my mind can finally shut down. It's like a lullaby. Nothing else has ever soothed me like the ocean does."

Perhaps this is true for you as well. Maybe you like the ocean. There is certainly something slightly hypnotic about watching, listening to and smelling it for me. Others prefer being in a forest under towering trees and staring up at a green canopy with sunlight shining through, the smell of pines wafting on the wind and birds chirping in the background. Maybe you prefer staring at a fire, hearing the snapping and popping and crackling as well as its distinctive smoky smell. There are all sorts of ways you can get a similar experience, but what this does is help shut your conscious mind down. All of these things help you get into a trance-like state and are forms of self-hypnosis that help you calm yourself down.

You'll notice that you are beginning to enter this state because you'll stop feeling the need to move around so much. Instead, you'll want to sit down, or stay in one place, and stare. Once you do, you'll also notice yourself taking deep breaths and feeling a sense of calm. This is a sort of self-hypnosis that you can purposely practice, to help induce a state of deep relaxation. If you want to learn more about this, try Googling "self-hypnosis for relaxation."

When you're grieving, you often stop breathing as deeply and lose that deeper sense of calm we can often tap into when we are more healthy and stable. If you can find places and ways that you are able to purposely stop yourself from focusing on your grief, even for short periods, and allow yourself to breathe more deeply, it can have extremely positive effects. This is because, while it may seem like a small thing, deep breathing helps tell your body (via your nervous system) that you can calm down and relax.

## DANCING WITH LIFE

After having been in Florida for some time, my headaches and pain slowly began to recede. The ocean worked her magic on me. I cried all the tears I needed to cry and took the time I needed to grieve. And then, eventually, I found that I didn't need to cry all the time anymore.

I began to look at my life and take stock. I recognized that although I couldn't replace him, some of the things that I missed with Marcelo's absence were things I could begin to find alternatives for, or manage. For example, although I have spent most of my adult life in the US and loved being here, one of the things I missed in Marcelo's absence was a connection to Argentina.

With him gone, I suddenly was missing a connection to my birthplace and Argentinian culture, so I decided to try going to some tango milongas. While Marcelo had always been athletic, he had never been a dancer, so we never considered trying lessons together.

With him gone, it suddenly became a possibility. I didn't expect to meet anyone through it, but did want to surround myself with my culture and begin to enjoy my body again. After having seen Marcelo have so much pain in his body, and having had so much pain myself, I wanted to reclaim my body as a place I could simply exist in. And enjoy.

Tango is a beautiful dance. But it is not simple. It is a dance that so fascinates people they often dedicate their lives to learning it. It gave me a way to build trust in my body and become close to men again long before I wanted to consider dating.

I should explain that I had taken some tango lessons four years earlier, when the kids gave me tango lessons as a present when I turned fifty. I kept putting off using the voucher they gave me with one excuse or another. At the time, my son was on a college exchange in New Zealand for six months and every time we talked, he would ask if I had started.

Eventually, he returned and I still hadn't started. The kids understood. Marcelo was ill and I felt guilty about "having fun," or doing anything, away from him. One summer Saturday morning, Ivan asked me again if I had started.

"No, not yet." I responded. "I keep meaning too, it's just with your dad and everything else I just haven't gotten around to it yet. I'm sorry, I really do want to."

"Mom, get in the car. I'm giving you twenty minutes. I've already checked. There's a class starting in an hour and you're going."

It was impossible for me to say no, because he knew I didn't have anything else planned, since we were going to spend the day together to welcome him back from New Zealand. It was an offer I couldn't refuse.

Although my heart was pounding and, if I remember correctly, I tried to insist I needed to mop the floor instead of going. He finally got me into the car and we went. When he saw how hesitant I was, Ivan joined the class with me.

Alexey, our teacher, smiled kindly at his first mother-son pair before clapping his hands to get everyone's attention. He started the lesson by telling us that we were going to learn how to walk again. Yes, in tango they teach you to walk again.

"This is silly," I thought to myself. "If I had started as a child then maybe I would have a chance, but I'm too old for this now."

I had almost decided to grab Ivan and slip out the back door, but then got caught up in watching how he was showing us to shift our weight onto the balls of our feet. He made it look easy and was gliding along the floor ahead of us effortlessly.

I couldn't replicate anything he was doing. I was wobbling all over the place in my heels. All we were trying to do was take a couple of steps forward and I was worried I might fall. It was one of the hardest classes I'd ever taken. Maybe tango was a mistake.

"Lead with your chest and push yourselves forward up from the ground through the balls of your feet. Now stride, stride, stride, stride!"

None of what he was saying made sense to me. Eventually, he came over, actually bent down beside me and literally put his hands on my feet to show me how I should be pushing my feet into the ground to help jettison myself forward. Suddenly I stopped wobbling and jumped almost a foot ahead easily and without almost any effort. I was hooked.

Ivan liked tango too, although not as much as me, and only dropped out when he had to go back to college in the fall. By then, he knew I felt comfortable with the teacher, Alexey. In fact, I loved it! I continued on with classes until Marcelo died.

Tango is certainly not a dance for everyone. It is highly dramatic and very intimate and takes years to learn the basics. I'm not suggesting that you might consider learning tango or even taking up another form of dance.

However, it is worth considering doing some form of movement or exercise. This is because, like with the forms of self-hypnosis in nature that I mentioned in the previous section, it helps take you out of your head and focuses you on something other than your emotions for short periods. This can be a very needed respite when you are grieving.

The added benefit of physical movement, and this is even more true of intense exercise, is that your body produces feel-good chemicals in response. This can help mitigate and balance some of your grief.

## GOING BEYOND IMAGINATION

In the previous chapter, I mentioned how some of Dr. Joe Dispenza's ideas had helped me. Initially, it was the aspect of meditation that I thought would get me distance from the pain. However, there is a key element to his ideas that I believe is what, finally, helped rid me of my pain once and for all.

When I started out doing his programs, they helped, but the pain didn't stop. What I hadn't understood at first was his key point: you need to do more than just visualize the future you want. You need to believe it and feel it into being.

That means, for me with my throat pain for example, I needed to go beyond just visualizing a time when I would have a life without it. Instead, I needed to begin to believe in a future when I could easily sing pain-free with friends. I would then concentrate on imagining that scenario and feel the joy I would experience in doing that.

Or, cheering loudly and without restraint at a soccer game. As part of that process, some of the work I did was about feeling the excitement, exhilaration and gratitude that my throat was no longer an issue for me, for an event that had not yet occurred. I repeated the experience and believed in that until it became a reality for me.

I'm not an expert in this, but understand that there is research out there that shows the brain doesn't differentiate between thoughts and reality. So, if you have very "real" thoughts and attach emotions to them as well, your brain responds the same way to them as it does to the things that actually happen to you. That is why these types of practices work.

You begin this "virtuous circle" by imagining something good happening to you, then you support it becoming reality by repeating it and feeling how good that experience will be, over and over again. Your brain doesn't know the difference, so it begins to tell your body to react and respond as if those things are true for you.

Obviously, there are limits to what you can manifest or make reality, but the worst that can happen with this is that you spend some time imagining good things happening to you during a difficult time in your life.

---

When you initially experience grief, it often overwhelms you and takes control of your mind, body, emotions and even life, completely. However, at a certain point, you need to begin to find ways to purposefully heal yourself. This often will mean learning new, sometimes unconventional methods or things, which allow you a break from your normal routines of thinking or feeling.

# 10

# THE NEW: FINDING NEW PURPOSE

I have spent most of this book so far writing about dying and grieving or healing. I want to spend the rest of this book talking about what it means to live again after a life-changing loss, such as that of a spouse.

## NEW PERSON

I think it is easy to forget that when a spouse dies, especially if you were together for any significant period of time and your lives were bound together, then part of the reason losing them can be so doubly devastating is because they often form a significant part of your identity. Then, when they die, the person you were only with them dies as well.

For example, many people only share aspects of sex, certain inner emotions, their children's development, and so on with their spouse. If you were together for five, ten, twenty years or more, then the person you were in those intimate moments you shared only with them is gone. That can be quite a significant part of yourself. For some, it can feel like their whole selves.

Many people don't understand that part of what they are grieving, with a lost spouse, is the loss of their own identity and memories. And at first, there are reminders of that loss everywhere.

Opening a drawer and finding a personal item of theirs might not just remind you of them, but also of how easily you used to live together. Of how you used to take for granted that you were in a relationship with someone who spent time lovingly creating an overly organized sock drawer early on Sunday mornings as you rolled your eyes behind their back and lazed in bed.

Or, you may see a photograph of you together. It may not just bring their face back to life for you, but also the event you two were at when it was taken. And, it could remind you that before your partner died, you used to love going out. That you used to be someone who was social. An extrovert. Now you can't imagine voluntarily going out to group events.

The idea of having so many people staring at you with pitying looks on their faces—or even worse, directly asking you how you are doing—fills you with dread. And reminds you that you don't feel like the same person you used to be. You stare at the smiling, innocent person you used to be in that photo and don't recognize yourself anymore. Is that really you, still?

You can't imagine feeling happy and relaxed at a BBQ anymore like you did back then. And, you remember you were the one who had insisted the two of you go. You were the "life of the party" and everyone laughed when you had to be dragged away at the end of the night. Not anymore. That person died when your partner did.

Similarly, reading an old postcard or text message with the in-jokes and special love language that you only used with each other. It reminds you that no one else knows how to love you in your special code anymore. All the things that used to make you laugh, and giggle and snort and feel understood… anyone else reading them now would just see gibberish. Nothing special.

Those moments are all triggers at first. Until, eventually, you begin to accept that you can still live, only you will need to adapt. It will need to be a different life than the one you expected and thought it was going to be. A life that maybe won't include BBQs and sock drawers and your silly, old codes, but one that will still be worth living. You may not even be sure what that life includes yet to make it worth living. A life that is waiting out there for you and needs to be discovered.

Your new life is for a new person. After deep trauma or grief, you are still emerging from your cocoon and are not what you used to be anymore. So, you will need to try new things. Don't be like *The Ugly Duckling*. Understand that you have become a swan and can't go back to the life you once led. Your grief will have transformed you so that your old life won't let you back in anymore, even if you bang and crash and try to force your way back in.

I like to see grief now as a time of cocooning. As if grief and loss stripped away the wings of my old life and turned me into a caterpillar for a period of time. However, eventually, I began to realize that I was not buried and had not actually died. I had to separate myself from Marcelo, and from the parts of my identity that I lost.

Perhaps it sounds stupid. To those who haven't grieved deeply I am sure it will, but I think those who have lost a spouse will understand: eventually, I had to accept that although it felt as if I had died alongside Marcelo, I hadn't. For me, it was only a metaphor. I was simply in a period of transition and needed to re-emerge from my cocoon, find my wings and figure out how to fly again.

## NEW EXPERIENCES

There is a certain freedom that comes with losing a spouse that I had only heard about in grief support groups and seen talked about on online forums (in terms of the guilt that many felt). About eighteen months after Marcelo's death, I finally felt it as well.

At a certain point in many people's journey, when they begin to realize that it is time for them to find their wings again, they begin to think back on their relationship and all the things they gave up for it. Even in the best of relationships and lives, you have to make choices and prioritize.

However, losing a spouse often creates a hole in most people's lives. A space that they suddenly find that they want to fill with new people or travel or hobbies. Some people function best in a relationship and so that is where they look first: sometimes it is a specific person, other times it is just another partner in general.

However, many others think about all the other things in life that they gave up to focus on their relationship. Whether it is a university degree or specific career, more friends, travel or a hobby, suddenly they have time for the things they always wanted to do. If you are still in deep grief, this might seem ridiculous or even sacrilegious. But, maybe just remember that there might come a time when your world will expand again.

A time when you no longer need to arrange your life around somebody else's absence or needs, and that starts to feel exciting. A time when you have the emotional and physical space to choose if you want to explore the world again. For example, you can choose to do things that your former partner was not good at, did not understand or enjoy, or never had time for.

You are now allowed to be selfish if you are still single. You likely have the luxury of exploring new experiences that are mainly dictated by your decisions or inclinations, now that you no longer need to take theirs into account. Even if you have children, being a parent requires a very different type of compromise than a partnership.

Regardless of how much you loved your partner, there were likely some things you would have liked to do but needed to adjust because of the course of your lives or how you chose to prioritize your relationship. That is likely no longer required.

When people coming out of periods of bereavement first realize that, they feel immense elation and freedom. Then guilt and often even anger. Many go on to explore new things and find out what suits them now, and suits the new life they want to develop.

As I said, one major way I did this, once I realized I had the freedom to do whatever I wanted, was to start dancing again.

Walking into a tango lesson for the first time with my son was scary. I wasn't sure what I should say to people about not being in a couple (nobody even asked). Should I just wear pants or a dress (didn't matter)? I felt silly in my heels. Experienced Argentine tango dancers wear three-inch heels. However, that first time at least I had my son with me.

When I decided to start going to tango milongas down in Florida (the formal evening tango dances, not classes), I didn't have Ivan with me cheering me on. I felt clumsy walking back into a tango environment. Even though I knew how to dance, the last time I tangoed had been before Marcelo had died.

Luckily I knew the milonga host, Denise, who was leading the class. She smiled at me when I entered. The music playing was classic tango music, familiar to me from youth, played in bars and homes all over Argentina. She waved me over and we chatted a bit before class began. I had phoned her ahead of time to explain my situation and had told her that I'd never been to a milonga before even though I was Argentinian.

"I'm glad you came tonight Sandra. I think you're the type of person who will adore milongas. I think they're probably in your blood. Just give it some time."

I shook my head, "Oh, I didn't take lessons for very long in New Jersey. I'm not very good at it. Even though I'm Argentinian, I never danced when I was younger."

She repeated a famous Argentine quote to me in Spanish. "No importa cuanto tango hay en tu vida, sino cuánta vida hay en tu tango." Translated, it means "It doesn't matter how much tango is in your life, but how much life is in your tango."

## NEW ROUTINES

Part of developing a new you, and a new life without your partner, means developing new routines for yourself. Instead of only trying to hold on to the old life I had with Marcelo, I decided to move to Florida close enough to the beach to swim in the ocean every day.

Or, at least that's what I thought I wanted to do. Once I got here, I realized that I don't actually want to swim in the sea every day for a variety of reasons. However, I do feel a need to be by the ocean every day so I try to go for a walk by it every morning.

I've noticed lately that there are an increasing number of influencers trying to give lists of "the perfect way to start your morning" on YouTube and Instagram. Many of them include getting up early and doing some meditation, then journaling. A lot of them suggest making your bed, as if that's a revolutionary idea!

I'm not sure that it really matters what you do except that, especially after a long period of grief or trauma, it helps if you can figure out something that reliably makes you feel good to start off your day.

I think it helps if it is something that feels easy to do and doesn't take too much effort. And then you start doing it every day, or as often as possible. From what I can see, that is one of the major ways that people begin to heal more quickly.

They figure out what makes them feel better. Simple, easy, non-harmful things. And then they do it. Over and over again. Day after day. For short periods. Something that takes twenty to thirty minutes at most.

Setting up a routine like that eventually helps to retrain our brains into remembering that life doesn't always feel painful and sad. That sometimes you can wake up to a smile. Because you are about to do something that feels good.

---

After losing someone you love deeply, your life can lose its direction and meaning. Where once your life flew and soared through the heavens, you find you can barely get off the ground anymore. Eventually, you need to find new ways to fly again. First though, you may need to accept that you need to make new wings for yourself. Different than, or at least modified from, the ones you had before.

# 11

# THE OPENING: LOVING

Once you begin to live again, often slowly with ups and downs and in fits and starts, something in you breaks open. Living means allowing yourself to be vulnerable. Living can be scary because living means loving.

## STEP-BY-STEP

I didn't start tango lessons thinking about relationships explicitly. But tango taught me a lot about intimacy and relationships. I hope after the death of a partner you are able to find a safe space, like tango was for me, that allows you to explore intimacy and relationships slowly, at your own pace on your journey back to love.

The first unexpected gift that tango gave me was touch. Of course I had watched tango hundreds if not thousands of times. But before I was actually held by someone that first time in a tango embrace, I hadn't thought about how close I would be to someone again.

More specifically, I hadn't really thought about the fact that a man would be drawing me into his body, pressing me up against his chest and holding me very, very close while we danced. That I would finally be hugged again in a close embrace for long minutes at a time. Marcelo and I had always been affectionate with each other and living alone, I often went weeks without touching another human being in any significant way.

After my first milonga, I went home and sobbed. That time it was not because of grief but because I had not realized how much I had missed being touched by other human beings. I was crying with relief and recognition. I had missed the intimacy of simply being close to other people. And, what a relief it was, after years of loss after loss after loss, to suddenly be given something I so desperately needed that I hadn't even realized I was missing.

Humans need touch and when a partner dies, this is something that many people report craving the most. If dance isn't for you, you can get similar benefits from massage, petting animals or even making pottery on a wheel.

I missed being cuddled by Marcelo but hadn't thought about how tango would fill that space in my life. It ended up filling a need for affection and physical intimacy, but in a non-committed and non-sexual way that I hadn't even known was important for my healing. I found that I loved being rocked gently during the dance. Perhaps, in some ways as well, it also recalled being rocked by my father as a child as he would walk with me back and forth trying to settle me at night.

The second gift tango gave me was that it helped me learn about chemistry before I began dating again. In tango classes, you often switch partners, one after another randomly in a circle. It is a bit like speed dating. You have about thirty seconds to greet each other before you move into the tango embrace and then start dancing.

In tango, the leader (usually a man but not always) is supposed to communicate what they want the follower to do mainly by angling their chest, driving their arm and moving backwards and forwards. It soon becomes clear that some people, who you think are physically attractive from afar, are often not as nice up close and you find you don't dance well with them at all.

However, others who you might not have looked twice at on the street can be incredible leaders you develop the most amazing chemistry and dance with. Having not dated much as a teenager aside from Marcelo, it taught me some important lessons about what was really important to pay attention to when I was ready to start dating again.

We are all different, but my suggestion is that you try to ensure you feel safe and go at a pace that feels manageable for you when you are exploring relationships and intimacy once more. Find other ways that allow you to fulfill some basic needs you have, such as being held or sharing your deepest thoughts with others, so that when you find a potential new partner, you are functioning as much as possible from a place of wholeness rather than neediness. So that a longing to replace your dead partner doesn't drive your choices for new relationships.

Tango also taught me about discipline. This is something that I know Marcelo had a lot of, but I had never applied systematically to my own life in the same way. However, to improve in tango you have to practice the same steps over and over again. Step after step. Back and forth. For years. Until you don't have to think about it anymore and your body just remembers.

Except, unlike when I was talking about your body remembering trauma (like Babette Rothschild's book title suggested in an earlier chapter), this time I am suggesting you purposely imprint muscle memory to create beauty.

After that first class, I kept going back to tango. Slowly, step-by-step, I learned how to walk again the tango way. It is a good metaphor for what happened in the rest of my life as well. Because, just as I was being taught to walk again in tango, I was also learning to "walk" again without Marcelo elsewhere in my life.

At first I was like a toddler, wobbling and hesitant. Needing encouragement and falling to my knees and crawling more often than not. But eventually I found my balance again. And then I became more confident. I started striding purposefully through my life but recognized that I needed to adapt to my new self and walk differently than I had before. Eventually, I began to run and remembered I had wings so I began to fly again sometimes, too.

The final major gift that tango gave me is appreciation. Marcelo was always the person who brought color into my life and gave me purpose, in a way. When he left, it wasn't just my grief that drained my world, it was that he had always helped me see things more intensely.

And then, those little nudges and tips and comments he always used to make were gone.

That's part of the reason my life suddenly turned gray, I think. I needed to find a way to brighten my world myself for the first time. To notice the tiny details and appreciate them by myself. Tango is a dance of details and small flourishes. To the uninitiated, most of what goes on at a milonga would be completely invisible.

For example, much of what is communicated between the leader and follower is not spoken. Even before they dance together. Even from across the room. It is traditional that a leader will begin their approach to a potential follower from afar.

They do this initially by making eye contact. They also might raise their eyebrows with a questioning "Hello, would you like to dance with me later?" If the follower is amenable, they will give a slight smile and nod their head. That is all.

Then, at some undetermined point, later in the evening, they both know that they will dance together. Sometimes they approach the follower immediately and ask them to dance in words, but not often.

In this way, tango helped me start to pay attention to the little things that are easy to overlook. Because most of our lives are made up of tiny, seemingly unimportant moments. Moments that are easy to miss while you are waiting for something special to happen.

For example, when I first started tango all I wanted was to actually dance. Eventually, I learned to savor and enjoy the entire culture and every moment of a milonga. The choosing of my dress and strapping on of my high heels. The formal greeting of people I knew when I entered the milonga room. The back and forth with leaders and their eyes. The watching of other dancers and the exhilaration of being amidst so many graceful swooping bodies, moving perfectly in rhythm together to the percussion of my childhood.

This is an important part of beginning to love the world and your life again: finding ways to watch it intensely. Times and places where you are partially being an observer but also partially involved. Not just an outsider but not completely taking part either.

Some people find they experience this most easily with family; watching their grandchildren, for example. You don't need to have a family or even join groups to do this. You can paint or run or find many things to do where you are concentrating on an activity but not having to focus on it all the time. In this way, you can observe others and enjoy more than just the "doing" but also the experience and the others taking part as well.

CONSCIOUS RESILIENCE

Learning to appreciate tiny things was a first step. The next thing I learned is to love what is. I think both those help you develop a sort of conscious resilience. But actually, if I'm honest, for a period at first I only wanted to introduce things into my life that would last because it felt that so much else that I had loved had gone.

For a while, I embraced the superficial "newness" in Florida. Maybe something within me knew I would need that to prepare for what was to come. My father died a couple of years after I moved to Florida, while I was with him visiting on a trip to Argentina.

Then, less than a year later in March 2020, I traveled to Argentina again, just after the pandemic was officially announced, and landed on the last flight allowed back just as everything was closed down. My mother then died shortly after. It was a lot of death in the space of three years: Marcelo, Apollo and both my parents. There were more people too that I won't list here, it gets exhausting.

After my mother died, I was stuck in Argentina during the pandemic. The airports were closed so I stayed in my parents' house for three months during those first fear-filled months. I was not able to work, as the international travel business I had at the time suddenly was no longer viable. Suffice to say, my business phone didn't ring for two full years.

Looking back, I know I had many blessed years in my life and then some extremely difficult years. I was forced to learn some very hard lessons quickly and brutally. I wish it had been easier for me at times, but am grateful for what I have had in my life and what I have learned.

Through all of this, one of the things I learned is to adapt. Resilience. Those three months could have sent me into a downward spiral of depression. They certainly weren't easy and were an extremely difficult time for me. But, by that point in my life I had decided to learn from the lessons life was giving me.

I didn't want to feel victimized by my life or loss anymore. So, I took what life dealt me and said "Thank you very much for the time I had with them. I am going to make time in my life to honor their memories and be sad but keep on living this time anyway."

Part of what makes life so hard is our expectations around what we think we should have, rather than what we are actually going through. When you stop thinking about the past or what you used to have and focus on the present, and appreciate where you are and what you have now, life becomes much easier, in my experience.

When my parents died, it was hard and I was devastated, but it didn't affect my sense of identity or expectations about the future in the way Marcelo's death had. Perhaps it would for other people whose relationship with their parents was more fraught or whose spouse was still alive.

But because I had already processed many of those issues with Marcelo's death, that might have come up if one of my parents had died first, it didn't strike at my heart in the same way. It wasn't that I loved them less. It was simply that I knew what to expect and how to navigate grief and loss this time around. I knew how to mourn them while still taking care of myself.

I also knew that I needed to focus on the loss of my career and mourn that as well. I knew I was resilient and could adapt, so wasn't powerless anymore in the way I had felt before. I didn't need to keep trying to control the future to fit into one mold of my expectations.

When you accept that what you once thought was going to be your future may no longer be possible, and open up to what is, then your life often blossoms in ways you never could have imagined.

That is what, slowly, began to happen for me. First, I began to explore for myself what else I could be doing. What else I had loved and how I could expand my horizons. Then I began to get support in doing this from others in order to maximize my success, such as working with a coach.

The one thing about losing a spouse is that it is a trial by fire. If you let it, it can transform your deep sorrow into a powerful new you who is able to take on the world and whatever it throws at you.

## LOVE LESSONS

Eventually, life will start giving you blessings again. It took what felt like years of hard work and managing through loss to come out the other side. But I did. I ended up with many new wonderful things and interests and people in my life. I have a new home, a new career. People who have become true friends.

And then I met George. A dear tango friend, Tullio, wanted to celebrate his birthday at a popular milonga that I had never been to. So I went. When I arrived, there were just a handful of familiar faces. Tullio was standing there with a few other friends so I went over to greet him. The rest of the people were all unfamiliar but seemed very friendly. There was a good atmosphere and I looked forward to a wonderful evening. Soon, we were all laughing and having a good time even before the dancing began.

Unlike other types of dance, at milongas the same people and couples often attend over and over again, for years. So, each milonga has its own distinct atmosphere and devotees. Many are very friendly with an almost familial atmosphere. Food, usually empanadas, and wine are often served with tables ringing the dance floor. Often groups of friends who have been attending a milonga for years will claim a table, or group of tables, as "theirs" and sit there every time they attend that milonga in the same place.

A man named George had attended the milonga we went to for Tullio's birthday for over ten years. Because he had been going there for so long, it meant that he knew every single person who usually attended. When I arrived, he noticed me right away.

He tells me now that he didn't even see me at first. His back was turned but he heard me laughing. He wondered who it was and only when he turned around to find out did he see me. It was a strange woman at "his" milonga! He liked my smile immediately and felt himself smiling in return.

He asked me to dance and, after a brief amount of small talk, exchanging our names, we moved onto the dance floor and he took me into the classic tango embrace. In Argentine tango, I talked about having chemistry with someone, and you find this out even before you get into the embrace. As soon as you start to come close to one another, you come into contact with the other person's energy.

For those of us who are sensitive to energy, the mixing of one's energy with another's determines if there is connection or not between dance partners. Two people may have good technical ability, and may be of a similar level, but if there is no energetic connection there, it shows, and its lack can be very clearly felt.

Energetic connections make the difference between an unforgettable dance or three very long minutes! With George, I felt at ease from the first moment. He has a soothing energy and, for me, it is always a pleasure to dance with him. During our first dance, I felt like I had known him for a long time.

Although with other men and dating, I had felt hesitant or scared or uncertain, it never felt that way with

George. Not at all. I felt at home with him from the first moment. I felt good. My body was clearly telling me that this was a safe person to be with because I felt calm around him. I could breathe. Deep breaths, like when I was walking on the beach watching the waves roll in.

Just like your body will tell you when something is wrong and it will try to save you the only way it knows how, by causing you pain to force an emergency that will change your life, it will also try to signal you when you find yourself in good places or around good people.

Lust is one thing, as we all know that type of chemistry usually signals a short-term attraction. After you have experienced grief or loss and are looking for people, places or things that are healthy for you, pay attention to the effect they have on your body.

They should not excite or stimulate you. Instead, when you find that you respond with deep breaths and become more relaxed and calm, then those are the people, places and things you should gravitate towards because it is your body telling you that there is nothing to fear. There you will be safe to love again.

After you lose a spouse and begin to emerge from a period of bereavement, you need to begin to live your life again. One of the important stages of beginning to live again is opening up and allowing yourself to love once more.

# THE LIGHT: DEVELOPING YOUR WISDOM

I wish that I could end this book by telling you that I understood everything about grief and was completely over losing Marcelo now. That I never felt lost or sad or uncertain anymore. But I do; the truth is I am still learning more about it and still miss him.

What I'm going to share with you in this last chapter are the ten lessons I think grief taught me. Maybe you can learn from these things too.

- **Give your loved one a "good death," even if it has to be retrospectively.**

Loss teaches us that death is a natural part of life. It is inevitable and happens regardless of what we do.

Although it feels wrong, death is not a mistake. That said, there are certainly better ways to die than others.

Some people and cultures are also more accepting and simply better prepared for death. Part of this, sometimes, is because they have a closer proximity to death than we do in the US and Western cultures in general. Another reason may be religious and spiritual beliefs.

- **Retreat from the world and let yourself be sad for a while, but then stop.**

At its most basic, grief is a recognition that you have lost someone or something you loved. That you will not be able to get them back and that you are going to have to find your way in the world without them from now on.

This means that you will need to discover how you accommodate feeling loss and sorrow in your life in the future. In some of the online forums I've browsed, some people report having problems dating. Many said that they had been told prospective partners were turned off by widow(er)s because they didn't want to have to compete with their dead spouses.

While this has never been a major issue between George and me, dating me was not always an easy process for him either, because he has still had to navigate my grief and accept Marcelo as part of my life. As someone dating a widow, he found it pivotal when we went together to visit Argentina for the first time. First, we went to visit my parents (who welcomed him). Then, I took him to Marcelo's family home where he met all of Marcelo's family as well. They welcomed him and told him stories about us and Marcelo.

For the first time, George felt as if Marcelo was finally revealed to him. Up until that point, Marcelo had been a bit of a fairy tale, I suppose. He had only been a figment of imagination, someone in the stories I told him. But then suddenly, he came to life in Argentina. While it had never been an issue for us, George had never truly understood until then, when he finally began to grasp things on a deeper level. Luckily for us, Marcelo's family were also very supportive and happy for me to move forward with another relationship. And we are the lucky ones. Many do not encounter such a supportive reception from their families.

Even when families are not the issue, to be fair, having some hesitancy about dating widow(er)s is realistic because some never stop grieving. They don't move beyond their sadness and never truly come back to life again. I honestly believe that is because, ironically, they are actually scared to let themselves truly feel their loss completely.

Because they never fully grieve, letting it flow through them with all its crazy force, they get stuck in a weird superficial cycle where they are trying not to be sad but then actually feel it more deeply because they will not admit it. They get stuck in a vicious cycle of feeling what they refuse to feel.

If you don't express grief, it takes over your life and begins to haunt your every waking moment. It's no wonder so many people are concerned about ending up in a relationship with someone who brings the ghost of their dead spouse everywhere they go. That's why you need to find ways to stop grieving, eventually.

One of the best ways, as far as I can tell, to get yourself to "stop" is to let yourself be brave enough to feel the full force of your sadness for as long as you need to, and trust that one day, something inside you will decide you have other things to do. That day will come. Let yourself grieve. Then find a way to save yourself by stopping.

- **Trust your body even when it is causing you pain.**

Our bodies very rarely lie to us. In fact, they usually are trying to do exactly what they think we need most, even when they are causing us pain. Let me write that again in ALL CAPITAL LETTERS and *italics*, just in case you didn't hear me.

**OUR BODIES ARE ALMOST ALWAYS TRYING TO HELP US EVEN WHEN THEY ARE CAUSING US PAIN.**

That means the last thing you should do when you have some unexplained and sudden pain is try to get rid of it. Instead, it is a warning sign. It is your body turning on a metaphorical smoke alarm to warn you there is something wrong.

Think about it. Why would you turn it off and carry on as if everything is normal when your metaphorical house (body) is about to burn down? Because this is exactly what we've been taught to do in modern society. We've been taught that we shouldn't have pain. That pain is bad. And, so when our body is trying to help us by alerting us that something is wrong, we shut it off.

Usually, our body starts warning us when there are initial small things going wrong, and we could have had a chance to address and solve them at that point. But, because we ignored it instead, and often felt proud of ourselves, instead of getting rid of our pain our body has to keep making it worse to try to get our attention. And, usually, we keep ignoring it and turning off the alarm.

This is usually what happens with grief as well. Many of us are scared, and don't want to go deep into sadness, so our body eventually needs to shut us down completely. It has to "burn the house down" to force us to deal with the things it initially tried to use a smoke alarm to let us know about.

- **Consciously mourn, and have rituals for remembering the person you lost.**

For thousands of years, the concept of a good death and consciously letting go of your loved ones through a series of rituals over time has been of crucial importance. When someone passes away without a good death, many people and cultures believe that their spirit cannot pass or rest and so haunts the living. This is how the concept of ghosts came into being. For that reason, there are many ways to help the living let go of the dead.

Ironically, one way to help ensure that your loved one does not become a ghost is to remember them and honor their spirit regularly. Spirits who have passed, who are loved and respected, but also honored as clearly dead and let go of from the land of the living, are understood in this way as being supported to pass to the "other side." Many religions and cultures believe this and allow for this to happen in various ways.

Even if you are not religious or spiritual, remembering your loved ones through ritual clearly has psychological benefits for you. It helps you get emotional and mental closure for the relationship and allows you to say goodbye over time. As many times as you need.

Mourning rituals help the living identify themselves as sad and needing space from others, but also help them contemplate death and what it means to die. If you are not sure what a good death means, there are many places which already have definitions and explanations. You might start with books on the topic, religious and spiritual organizations, grief counselors, hospices, death doulas, celebrants and funeral homes.

- **Listen to your breath.**

One of the things that happens when you become sad is that you often lose touch with that inner sense of calm you may have had before you lost the person you loved.

One way to find your way back to places, people and things that can help center you, especially when you feel as if you have lost everything and everyone that makes sense in the world, is to listen to your breath.

Your breath is like a compass that will never steer you wrong. When you are in the right place or around people who are safe, it will know, and suddenly you will find your lungs opening up and wanting to take deep breaths again. Your body will need to breathe in a way it hasn't for a long time.

Notice when your lungs suddenly start to open up again and try to keep going back to the people, places and things where your body likes to breathe.

- **Risk the unknown.**

One of the things George has always noticed about me is that I don't shy away from doing hard things. I make hard decisions when necessary and risk the unknown even when it feels difficult.

This is what I think has allowed me to navigate so much grief over such a short period. I've been willing to go places and try things where I wasn't sure what the outcome would be. For example, starting a publishing company like this. Who knows what the outcome will be, but it keeps me engaged and curious and interested in life. What is going to happen next?

This doesn't mean that I have to put myself in danger or try things that feel unmanageable, or even do them all by myself without help. What it means is that there is wisdom in continuously seeking to go beyond your comfort zone, even after you have been hurt and want nothing more than to stay safe.

- **Move.**

Scientists talk a lot about "fight or flight" with animals. You could assume that when you are fighting or fleeing, then, that it is a bad thing. However, they have discovered that the animals who freeze are the ones who die. They are the ones who have given up because their bodies have gotten so overwhelmed they cannot save themselves anymore.

While there is a stage of grief where you need to cocoon, there will also come a time when you need to get moving again. Move in whatever way feels natural to you. Maybe you actually need to move house like me. Or jump around your kitchen to punk music in your pajamas, when no one is looking, shaking your fist angrily and yelling at God for letting your spouse die. Who knows how you'll need to move after a period of bereavement? Grief makes you do weird things. Try something. You'll figure it out.

- **Let love in.**

It's important to let love in again eventually as well. Allow love to enter your life in as many ways as you can after you've survived the trauma of loss and grief. After I met George, we soon started dating and quickly became serious.

My kids weren't so sure about me finding someone to 'replace' their dad, though, and wanted to meet him to check him out. Meeting adult children, and getting their acceptance, is always an important stage of any relationship. It is doubly so when this involves a widow(er). Luckily, we had a positive experience at our first meeting.

That's not to say that it was easy. We were all nervous before the event itself and my kids thoroughly "analyzed" George—before they even met him, from what I had told them in advance—and then afterwards as much as they could. They talked about what he wore, what he said, how he acted and stood and smiled. And still, he passed.

They gave him the green light and told me, "Mom, we're glad you found each other. We sense he is a good man."

I could see that they were just as scared as I had been, but at some point, just as I did, they decided to stop judging and just let love in. Something death teaches us is that the people we love will not necessarily stay with us forever and that we need to appreciate them and support their happiness when they are around.

I could see that's what they were trying to do with George and me. First, by trying to ensure he was good enough and then, by letting go and just allowing us to be together even though he wasn't their dad.

- **Remind yourself that you can survive this.**

After something horrible like the death of a spouse knocks us off our chosen course and pedestal, it can make us feel powerless. It can make us wonder how we were ever strong and able to live life without breaking down every hour (or ten minutes).

Sometimes, you end up staring at photos of yourself and believing that you will never be strong or normal or okay again. In some ways, that is true. You will probably never be able to completely repair yourself so that you forget the pain you have felt.

However, grief is one of the ways life makes us more compassionate and stronger, because of the way it transforms us. It is often a hard and cruel teacher but we never forget the lessons we learn from it. And, at its most basic, if you truly let grief teach you it will help you become a survivor. Someone who is resilient and wise.

- **Your life can become something beautiful even after deep trauma or sorrow.**

In the midst of deep grief and sorrow, we usually become the smallest, saddest, ugliest versions of ourselves. It is easy to be ashamed and feel unlovable. In those darkest moments, we often can do little more than bury ourselves and moan about our pain. It's rarely a pretty sight. It feels as if we will never be worthy of good or beautiful things in our lives again because all we can do is cry and wander around aimlessly.

And yet, eventually that process somehow often leads us to develop a depth and an understanding that we didn't have before. A knowing that sometimes makes us even more attractive and relatable than "before." Some even call it wisdom.

---

Grief and bereavement are never easy processes to undergo. However, you can learn wisdom and find love and beauty again, even after grief has turned your world black.

# LEAVE A 1-CLICK REVIEW!

Customer Reviews

★★★★★ 15

5.0 out of 5 stars ▾

| | | |
|---|---|---|
| 5 star | | 100% |
| 4 star | | 0% |
| 3 star | | 0% |
| 2 star | | 0% |
| 1 star | | 0% |

Share your thoughts with other customers

Write a customer review

IT WOULD MEAN THE WORLD TO ME IF YOU COULD
WRITE A BRIEF REVIEW ON MY BOOK. THANK YOU!

# EPILOGUE

Now that I have finished telling you about my darkest days, and sharing some of what I learned, you may be wondering where I am now. I know that I would want to know that about someone else.

I am still in Florida. After moving here from New Jersey, I found that this place felt like my new home and have settled here. My life isn't perfect though. I still have good days and bad days.

Honestly, there are still days when I miss Marcelo and want to bawl my eyes out suddenly and unexpectedly, even though I have a new partner who I am very pleased to be with, love dearly and who treats me well.

George knows that Marcelo is still present in my life that way and doesn't worry about it.

It was interesting to me to find out that he isn't threatened when Marcelo "returns" and is even the one who suggested I write this book. He thinks I am the woman I am because of my grief, not despite it. I am proud of George's confidence in this and appreciate his loving support. I don't have to hide that part of myself with him. That's a true gift in any intimate relationship. He wants to see me as I am, not who he thinks I should be.

In most ways, I would say I am living a happy and fulfilling life. I am doing things I love. A major part of what I had to learn to do initially, after moving here, was to stop trying to be good at things that were Marcelo's strengths or what we did well together, especially in business, and focus more on that which I excelled at on my own.

For example, once I figured that out (the pandemic gave me a huge push in this direction as it completely stopped my old travel business in its tracks for a period), I found that my business life started bringing me more joy. Letting go of solely focusing on my travel business was hard, especially after having so much other loss. I don't know that I would have done that willingly if "life" hadn't insisted. But life seemed to want me to begin anew once down here in Florida. So, I did.

Now, I try to start my day with a brief walk on the beach. I find that nothing sets the tone better for me than having some sort of contact with nature. I especially love seeing the ocean and the rising sun every day. It is something I am always so very grateful for and it makes me smile. What a beautiful way to start my days! I love it here and am so glad my crazy grief pushed me to come to the shore.

Then things get busy for me. I divide my day between my travel business and producing Spanish content for my online platform *Hola Fortuna,* which is soon to become my English online publishing house as well. There, I share experiences and information to motivate women through the challenges of midlife regarding kids, aging parents, jobs, preparing for a stable financial future, etc. I see it as my legacy in a way, where I can share all the things it took me a lifetime to learn (and am still learning) in short Spanish videos and in English ebooks. Hopefully this is just the first of many.

I spend a significant amount of time traveling for work and pleasure. My kids live in different states, so I make sure to see them often. When my son recently got married, he asked me to dance a tango for his mother-son dance. I was deeply honored. He had not taken

182 | SANDRA CAMPONOGARA

classes since those early days with Alexey when he was still in college. We coached him for a couple of hours and then danced, to a cheering crowd, the most memorable "Por Una Cabeza" that I will ever dance in my life. I felt the legacy of my ancestors passing on to the next generation, celebrating our roots and basking in the pure joy of the moment. If there was ever a time that Marcelo came back to watch us, I think he must have then.

I also still organize group travel vacations to the USA and Argentina a couple of times each year through my twenty-two-year-old business, InterConnect Travel. As I finish writing this book in August 2022, for example, I am very excitedly preparing a tango trip to Argentina in September.

As a tango fan, I have put everything in this tour that I would want if I was a paying customer visiting Argentina for the first time and wanting to attend as many of the best milongas as possible. It will be an epic tango and travel extravaganza! To be honest though, I'm not sure if I do it more for the clients or myself, because I always have such a good time. All I know is that I expect to fully enjoy myself alongside them! One of the perks of the job.

I also spend quite a bit of time writing. It is an old passion of mine. As a teenager, my father always thought I would be a writer or journalist because I was constantly taking notes and documenting things. Here's to you, Dad!

I get overly excited about learning new things and doing what I love, so I can get exhausted sometimes. This means I have had to learn to take care of myself more than I used to. This is both a reminder that I am getting older and also a leftover from the grief, showing me how I need to pay attention to nurturing my body and myself more than I did previously.

What I can honestly say now is that I have learned to bless my challenges: they have been my path to wisdom. That is one of the reasons I am writing this book. One day, I hope a long time from now as my soul prepares to leave this Earth, I want to look back and feel that I have touched others' lives in a positive way. I want to help show people how they can transform the difficult times in their lives as well.

For that reason, I offer this book to you in the hope that it will give you something positive to support you on your journey with grief.

**My gift**
*To You!*

# THE HEALING JOURNAL
## 6 POWERFUL STRATEGIES TO HELP YOU
## COPE WITH GRIEF

>> Scan the QR to Download your free Healing Journal <<

# RESOURCES PAGE

Dispenza, J. (2019). Becoming Supernatural: How Common People Are Doing the Uncommon (2nd ed.). Hay House Inc.

Rothschild, B. (2000). The Body Remembers: The Psychophysiology of Trauma and Trauma Treatment (Norton Professional Book) (Illustrated). W. W. Norton & Company.

Printed in Great Britain
by Amazon

27486828R00106